DISCARD

UNCIVIL WAR

UNCIVIL WAR

The Struggle Between Black Men and Women

ELSIE B. WASHINGTON

THE NOBLE PRESS, INC.
CHICAGO

Printed in the United States of America

Library of Congress Cataloguing–in–Publication Data

Washington, Elsie B.
    Uncivil War: struggle between black men and women/Elsie B. Washington

    p.   cm.
    Includes bibliographical references and index

    1. Afro–Americans—Marriage   2. Man–Woman Relationships—United States
    3. Afro–American Men—Psychology   4. Afro–American Women—Psychology

                                                    92–051079
                                                    CIP

ISBN 1–879360–25–X: $24.95

For my mother, Kathleen Peterson Erby

ACKNOWLEDGMENTS

THIS BOOK COULD NOT HAVE BEEN COMPLETED WITHOUT THE encouragement, support, friendship and assistance of a great many people; they have my gratitude and thanks. Among them: my agents Charlotte Sheedy and Denise Stinson; my editor Janet Cheatham Bell; Leah Jarrett, Samuel L. Jones, Glendoria C. Jones, James E. Peterson, Sharon Sam, Charles Wartts, Jamii Wartts and family, Kamau Seitu, C. Sade Turnipseed, William Kwamena–Poh, my sisters and brothers at *Essence* Magazine, Ruth Manuel–Logan, Judy Watson Remy and the Colored Girls, Yvonne Books–Little, Lee Abramson, Michelle Francis, Delmar Newby, Fikisha Cumbo, Alric Daly, Martha Bright, Sandy Bright and the Circle of Sisters, Angela Thorton, Jesse D.A. Taylor, Lester Sloan, Martha Fay, Sheila Colon, Joy Rankin, Charles Kaiser, Ernestine Seaborn, Willie Erby and The Prince–Peterson clan rooted in Hartsville, S.C. I also want to thank those people who were interviewed for this book in St. Louis, Washington, D.C., New York, Chicago and Oakland although their stories could not be included.

PREFACE

I HAD THOUGHT AT ONE POINT THAT THERE SHOULD BE NEON stickers on the front of this book declaring, "This book is not about man bashing!" and "This book is not about woman bashing!" I want readers to know from the start that the book doesn't indulge in that—it's much too easy to make sweeping generalizations that denigrate black men or black women. Besides, there's always a long line of people happy to do that dirty deed for us.

So I've tried to avoid bashing any group as a whole, although I do have a few things to say about public figures who seem to have made careers out of making black men or black women look bad. In a time of crisis, we don't need that!

The strain, the struggle between black men and women is much too serious to spend time airing hurtful, untrue, tired accusations. It's too important an issue to use this opportunity to tear down one side or the other. What's called for, I believe, is a recognition that we are at war; a balanced, in-depth look at how this war is being played out and how it affects the entire black community; what its underlying causes are and what efforts are being made to resolve the conflict.

Uncivil War: The Struggle Between Black Men and Women also looks at popular literature and film images on the subject and current events that revolve around it, such as the Anita Hill–Clarence Thomas case. Men and women offer their first person stories of relationships and black professionals—counselors, therapists and others—who work with individuals and couples give their analysis of the Uncivil War and the chances for peace. Finally, the book looks at some of the many programs nationally that are actively working to end the war.

It would be misleading to say that this book has the ultimate solution to the struggle. The solution is in many of the things that are said here by men and women themselves, by the experts, by grassroots programs that have made a solution their priority. But are we willing to hear what they have to say and begin to act on their ideas and recommendations? Have we become so used to warring that we believe it's an acceptable way of life? I think not.

We must end the Uncivil War between black men and black women and we need to do whatever it takes to do it. It is only then that we will be able to move forward as individuals, as couples, as a people.

—E.B.W.

CONTENTS

CHAPTER ONE

THE MARCH TO WAR

J ACQUELINE, A 43–YEAR–OLD OFFICE MANAGER FROM Detroit, has been married and divorced four times. Her first union ended after four years because her husband had become both physically and verbally abusive. Her second marriage lasted only a year, but Jacqueline's third, to a successful pharmacist, lasted somewhat longer. It ended only when her waning passion for her husband led her into the arms of another man. He was eventually to become her fourth husband. Yet five years later, they too, divorced.

Donald is a 25–year–old machine operator from Syracuse, New York. He is married to a white woman, but maintains that he did not go out consciously looking for one. "The way I look at it," Donald explains, "I just happened to fall in love with a Caucasian woman."

Denise, 37, is a Chicago–based talent scout. She has never been married, is not currently involved in a relationship and has not been for some time. She admits to being angry with black men, and believes that respect between black men and women is something that needs to be earned. "I don't give a brother, or a sister for that matter, respect just because they are black," she states. "People have to prove themselves worthy of respect. Most so-called 'brothers' will screw you over quicker than white people will."

John, a single, 35–year–old investment banker from New

York, has never been married. He also has not dated for over a year because his last three relationships, instead of providing him the "comfort and balance" he was seeking, only served to increase the already high level of tension and stress in his life. John admits that he prefers to date exciting women who are "high maintenance and slightly psychotic." He does not, however, feel that this is a major cause of his troubles on the love front. The real problem, he contends, is that "too many sisters expect men to pay for all of the sins of their previous boyfriends."

Like John, Faye, a 32–year–old clerk–typist has never been married and is currently not dating anyone. Faye says she is discouraged at her dating prospects based upon the "mess" that she sees her four sisters and her girlfriends going through. "It's not that there aren't any black men out there," says Faye, "but it seems that so many of them are violent, using drugs, lack ambition or are ego–maniacs. Or, all of the above."

Jacqueline, Donald, John, Denise and Faye are just a few of the many African American men and women interviewed for this book. Disappointed and often angry, these black men and women typify the millions of African Americans engaged in a long–running, and seemingly escalating battle between the sexes. A battle that can be accurately described as an "uncivil war" with slander, condemnation, finger–pointing, adultery, physical abuse, abandonment and more as the weapons of choice.

There have always been tension and conflict between the sexes of all races, but for African Americans, the discord has reached crisis proportions. Today, according to black sociologist Larry Davis, author of the best–selling book, *Black and Single,* two of every three black marriages end in divorce. In addition, according to sociologist William Julius Wilson, 22 percent of all married black women are currently separated from their husbands. What's more, African Americans are the only major ethnic group in America in which more adults are single than married.

Still, the soaring divorce rate among black Americans is just the tip of the iceberg. Most African Americans—yes, men and women—genuinely desire to establish and maintain a meaningful, loving relationship with another human being. To love and be loved is among the most basic of human needs. The inability to achieve this desire, however, along with the emotional pain and internalized anger of previous failed relationships, places tremendous pressure on a person both emotionally and spiritually. And while it's impact may be unquantifiable, there is no doubt that the Uncivil War contributes to the incidence of domestic violence, child abuse, alcoholism, drug use, poor physical health, depression and suicide presently afflicting the black community.

Most African Americans, however, do not need a recitation of grim statistics to see that an Uncivil War is raging. The visual and verbal indicators of this conflict can be seen and heard everywhere. The black male–female relationship struggle has been the focus of countless magazine articles, church and convention symposiums, rap music lyrics and many books and films written or produced by African American artisans. Indeed, it seems as if anywhere you listen, be it to the media, around the barber or beauty shop, at the mosque, the church or school, on the job, or at social gatherings, men and women are expressing anger and frustration with their counterparts of the opposite sex.

THE UNCIVIL WAR IS TELEVISED

GIL SCOTT–HERON, A BLACK POET AND MUSIC COMPOSER, once wrote: "The revolution will not be televised." And while that sentiment may still hold true with respect to the revolution, it unfortunately is not so for the Uncivil War. The media in all its forms—television news and talk–shows, newspapers, magazines and talk–radio—provide African Americans with constant and painful reminders that the turmoil is unending.

Media coverage includes frequent "war stories" about domestic violence, single parent families, infidelity and divorce. They also include pitiful reports about the youngest victims: Abandoned newborns, poor, malnourished and physically abused black children, throw–away kids and suicidal preteens.

In the media, the most attention–grabbing depictions of the Uncivil War are seen in the head–to–head clashes between black men and women of prominence. The sensationalized Clarence Thomas and Anita Hill confrontation, for example, not only captivated black America, but also the world. This feud showcased a black male judge and a black female law professor. It also featured a committee of very undistinguished U.S. Senators debating the significance of alleged pubic hairs on a Coke can, not to mention "Long–Dong Silver" adult films.

Despite the pervasive, near circus atmosphere, the issues that arose from the Thomas confirmation hearings—sexual harassment, vindictiveness, black unity, black sexuality, sexism and interracial marriage—were indeed serious and central to the Uncivil War. Across America, black men and women chose sides. They quickly formed strongly–held opinions not only about Hill and Thomas, but also concerning the host of related issues. Some black women saw Clarence Thomas as representative of "the stereotypical professional black male" who, they believe, yearns for white women. Some black men perceived Anita Hill as representative of "the stereotypical professional black female" who, they believe, is cold–hearted and vindictive. Other black men and women quarreled over the definitions of sexual harassment and sexism, while others hotly debated the impact of feminism on black male/female relationships. For most African Americans, it was virtually impossible not to have an opinion on these and related matters since everywhere one went, Hill and Thomas were being vehemently discussed.

The infamous 1988 Barbara Walter's television interview with then–heavyweight boxing champion Mike Tyson and his wife, Robin Givens, also galvanized the black community. To many African Americans, one of the most visible black men in the country had been verbally knocked out—some say castrated—on national television by a black woman. But to others, a beautiful black woman who was being brutalized at the hands of yet another beast of a black man, was telling her story.

Newly reelected Washington, D.C. Mayor Marion Barry did not have the benefit of a prime–time Barbara Walter's interview, but he did make front–page news. The FBI had been after Barry for years, but it was not until a black woman cooperated with them that they succeeded in getting their man. Again, the African American community split in their opinions on the Barry case. Although he was an admitted adulterer and drug user, for many black males, the most paramount issue was that yet another black woman had been key to bringing down one more high–profile black man.

Another high–profile politician, Congressional Black Caucus member Mel Reynolds found himself going toe to toe with two Black women: Beverly Heard and Andrea Zopp. Heard has accused Congressman Reynolds of having sex with her when she was only sixteen; Zopp, a prosecutor for the State of Illinois, has vowed to send the Congressman to jail for sexual misconduct. The coverage of this trial, which began in August of 1995, has dominated the front pages of the state's major newspapers. Many of the paper's readers found humor in the detailed reports of sexual acts, penis sizes, crotch–less panties, masturbation, "threesomes" and office strip teases. But for most African Americans, this public confrontation between an "oversexed" and "adulterous" black public official, a "cold, tough" black female prosecutor and a "wild, gold digging" black teenager was sad and disheartening.

Other highly publicized events that symbolized and helped perpetuate the Uncivil War include Tyson's controversial conviction for the rape of Miss Black America Pageant contestant Desiree Washington; Gangsta' rap artist Dr. Dre's attack on former TV show host Dee Barnes in a Hollywood nightclub because he thought she had "dissed" him on the air; the demise of Julian Bond's political career brought on by a black woman's assertion that she had used cocaine with the former Georgia state senator; Whoopi Goldberg's taking on the entire black community in support of her white boyfriend in black-face, Ted Danson; former NBA star Wilt Chamberlain's "admission" that he had slept with over 20,000 women and that he preferred white women because he thought they were better lovers; the arrest of NFL legend Jim Brown for alleged-ly beating a black woman; sexual harassment charges leveled by a black woman that led to the firing of NAACP executive director Benjamin Chavis; and of course, the never ending O.J. Simpson murder trial.

The mass media has not been the sole entity to focus on the negative aspects of black male–female relations. Some African Americans themselves have amassed small fortunes and con-siderable notoriety by trashing black male–female relation-ships. The lyrics of Gangsta' rapper's such as Luke Campbell's 2 Live Crew and N.W.A. (Niggers With Attitude) routinely label black women as greedy, sex–driven bitches, and scan-dalous "hoes." Even worse, some rappers feel the need to act out their sexist lyrics in real life. Top rappers such as Flavor Flav of Public Enemy, Snoop Doggy Dogg, and Tupac Shakur, Janet Jackson's co–star in *Poetic Justice,* have been arrested for various felony offenses including sexual assault and sodomy. Unfortunately, their bizarre behavior and mean–spirited lyrics seem only to boost sales of their albums, which, interestingly enough, are purchased heavily by young white males.

Gangsta' rap, however, is not the biggest profiteer of the Uncivil War. A black woman singlehandedly launched one of the largest surprise assaults of the war. In 1990, author Shaharazad Ali self– published *The Blackman's Guide to Understanding the Blackwoman.* The book was an immediate hit. The title appeared on black bestseller lists for almost two years; while Ali ran, sometimes in a chauffeur driven Rolls Royce, all over the country promoting her message and hawk-ing her book.

In *The Blackman's Guide to Understanding the Black-woman,* Shaharazad places the blame for the crisis in black relationships squarely upon the shoulders of black women. Her graphic depictions of some black women were shocking. She characterized black women as scheming, unkempt, sex–crazed, devious, disrespectful of black men and adulterous. Black women whom Ali labeled "high–class," were described as "rats who act like a dog while purring like a cat." And while many black women assumed that the primary audience for Ali's book would be less educated young men, several professional women interviewed reported that they knew black men among their peers who not only read the book, but who also gave them a copy. One of these was Janet, a book editor from Chicago who said, "He gave me the book, I read enough to be insulted and returned it. That ended our relationship."

In addition to Ali, other black writers have focused on the Uncivil War. Author Terry McMillan's blockbuster novel, *Waiting to Exhale,* explored the difficulty that some black women have in finding suitable partners and maintaining stable relationships. The black men featured in this fictional account ranged from negligent to nurturing, but with a discernible emphasis on the abusive. Many Black men denounced McMillan's story as "man–bashing," but women overwhelm-ingly embraced it as "realistic."

More recently, another bombshell dropped into the fray when gay Atlanta writer E. Lynn Harris' book, *Just As I Am* was published. In this novel, a black man dumps his fiancee when he "discovers" that he is bisexual. His fiancee subsequently falls in love with another man, who ironically had been her for-mer fiance's male lover.

The Uncivil War is also the preeminent subject matter of many black films. The movie *Poetic Justice* by John Singleton comes complete with castrating, gold–digging and angry black women, as well as images of impotent, "doggish," violent and gay black men. Two of filmmaker Spike Lee's offerings of recent years portrayed black men enamored of white women, and desperate black women putting up with dishonest, unfaithful black men. Eddie Murphy's *Boomerang* cast Robin Givens as a non–commitment–minded, self-absorbed, professional black woman. Murphy himself deftly delivered in his role of a successful "ladies man" looking for the perfect woman who also needed to have perfect feet.

What is most disturbing about these portrayals of black men and women are not that they exist. (There are, in fact, black men and women who mirror the depictions found in books, films, and rap lyrics.) The problem is the lack of a balanced representation. Whether in the news or in fictional accounts, negative portrayals of black relationships and related issues abound. While representations of positive black couples are, if not rare, not widely circulated or promoted. As a result, far too many African Americans have come to regard the negative portrayals as representative of the majority of black men and women.

WHERE DID THINGS GO WRONG?

RELATIONSHIPS BETWEEN BLACK MEN AND WOMEN WERE not always this strained. Today's alarming instability, according to sociologist Andrew Billingsley, is a very recent and rapidly escalating phenomenon. In his landmark study, *Climbing Jacob's Ladder: The Enduring Legacy of African–American Families,* Dr. Billingsley wrote: "For the 100–year period between the end of slavery and the aftermath of World War II, the structure of African American family life was characterized by a remarkable degree of stability. Specifically, the core of the traditional African American family system has been the nuclear family; composed of husband, wife and their own children. Divorce was rare and couples stayed together till the death of a spouse. As late as 1960, when uneducated black men could still obtain good–paying, blue–collar jobs in the industrial sector, 78 percent of all black families with children were headed by married couples. By 1978, only 64 percent of African American families with children were headed by married couples. This declined steadily to 48 percent by 1980, and to 39 percent by 1990."

The marked decline in the stability of black relationships, as well as a corresponding but less dramatic crisis in white relationships has been the focus of much debate and study. A number of explanations for the dilemma have been put forth by experts, including family therapists, political scientists, sociologists and theologians. The all–encompassing nature of this quandary, however—the fact that it impacts the poor and the wealthy, the educated and undereducated, young and old, the traditional and non-traditional relationship–minded alike—makes its analysis complex at best. It suggests that there is no one factor, but instead, an interaction of a number of social, economic, cultural and spiritual influences that fuel the continuance of the Uncivil War.

African Americans are "depressed, oppressed, unemployed, underemployed, angry and without hope." These are the elements most often cited by black family and policy experts as to why black men and women are at war with each other. In this section, we will examine how broader societal factors and circumstances influence black relationships, while in Chapter 2 the text will discuss how day–to–day behavior among individuals adds to the divisions between black men and women.

THE WHITE
CONSERVATIVE SMOKESCREEN

DESPITE THE ABUNDANCE OF AFRICAN AMERICAN AUTHORITIES qualified to address the issue from a black perspective, the hypothesis explaining the decline of the black family generally cited by mass media and white public policy makers comes from conservative white males. In fact, the often echoed, non–scientifically–based assumptions of Ronald Reagan's "favorite" sociologist, Charles Murray have become, for many black and white Americans alike, the gospel truth.

Conservative sociologists like Murray blame feminism and welfare, along with the "sexually amoral and irresponsible behavior of African–Americans," for the demise of the black family. Women today, confused by radical feminist theory, they argue, want to usurp the man's traditional role as head of the household. And as long as welfare pays black women will just stay at home, have babies and collect their checks. Black women, conservatives want us to believe, prefer the "generous" support of the state to a black husband or partner.

Media images to the contrary, most AFDC recipients are white and the average AFDC–dependent family has fewer children than the average American family. And despite the fact that in 1990 the average monthly welfare check for a family of three was a paltry $377 a month, in his book, *Losing Ground*, sociologist Murray exclaimed, "Worst of all, they didn't stop having babies after the first lapse. They kept having more. The most flagrantly unrepentant seemed to be mostly black, too."

Continuing his literary diatribe, Murray branded the alarming percentage of black men out of work as *voluntary*. In other words, it was a moral issue as opposed to a structural defect in America's economy. "The hardcore unemployed," Murray wrote, "were not people who were being rebuffed by job interviewers." Instead, he suggested, they "lacked ambition." Never before had America, Murray added, "witnessed such a large–scale voluntary withdrawal from the labor market by able–bodied males." Not so surprisingly, the conservative solution offered to resolve the black family crisis was as simple–minded as was their analysis: Eliminate welfare and return to "traditional family values."

Contrary to the conservative theory on feminism, all of the black women interviewed for this book appeared to be quite "traditional" in their attitudes toward male–female relationships. Most of them agreed that a husband should still be head of the household. They expressed no discomfort with their husband or significant other leading, just as long as their opinions were sought and respected and the man knew where he was going.

Elaine, a 49–year–old divorcee, was fiscally the most successful of the black women queried. Being the owner of a real estate firm, which manages the largest black–owned building complex in her city, she has to be assertive and in charge. She does not, however, prefer to be that way in a romantic partnership. "As long as everything was fine," she says regarding her 16–year marriage, "I didn't mind being submissive—being a 'traditional' wife. I know that I am intelligent and don't have to tolerate anything that I don't want to in a relationship. But I enjoy letting a man take the lead. I have no problem with that as long as I trust and respect him."

Studies conducted on the state of the black family also reveal that the conservative assertions that feminism and welfare are the root causes of its disintegration are unfounded and, as some would suggest, intentionally misleading. In his book, *The Truly Disadvantaged*, William Julius Wilson submits that "In the absence of systematic empirical data the effect of the feminist movement on the marital dissolution of women...can only be assumed." Dr. Wilson and Harvard sociology professor David Ellwood agree that the conservative claim that welfare leads to family breakups is also without merit. "Welfare simply does not appear," claims Dr. Ellwood, "to be the underlying cause of the dramatic changes in family structure of the past few decades."

THE BLACK PERSPECTIVE ON THE CRISIS

A REAL CATALYST FOR THE BREAKDOWN OF THE BLACK FAMILY structure is economics. More specifically, the lack of employment opportunities for black men. High–paying blue–collar jobs have all but disappeared due to an epidemic of plant closures in the United States. These closures are largely the result of the exportation of American jobs to cheaper overseas labor markets. According to black author David Driver, in the 1980s approximately 500,000 U.S. jobs were exported to Mexico's free trade zone alone where wages average less than $2 per hour. By the late 1980's, Driver details in his book, *Defending the Left*, "a full 29 percent of America's 'foreign imports' came from plants owned by American corporations." Largely as a result, by 1990, 32 percent of black men in their prime productive years, aged 20 to 44 were without work. Quoting Dr. Wilson, "...the percentage of black men who are employed dropped from 80 percent in 1930, to 56 percent in 1983."

The impact of this mass unemployment on the black family structure is clear. "The relationship between joblessness and marital instability," says Dr. Wilson, "is well established in literature. Moreover, available evidence supports the arguments that among blacks, increasing male joblessness is related to the rising proportions of families headed by women." In his book, *Poor Support,* Dr. Ellwood's conclusions concur with Dr. Wilson's. "There is accumulating evidence that part of the problem for young black men has been a lack of jobs. The evidence also points strongly to the possibility that the structure of the black family is suffering because of the weak performance of young men in the labor market."

Conversely, black women appear to have an easier time finding employment. According to Children's Defense Fund director Marian Wright Edelman, in the late 1980s there were 12 million more white men in the labor force than white women. At the same time, for the first time in the history of the United States, the average number of black women employed exceeded the average number of black men who also had jobs. With "more black men in prison than attending college," says sociologist Davis, there are far more black women obtaining college degrees and procuring high–paying careers in corporate America than black men. Currently, there are three black women on America's campuses for every two black males. Some college educated black males complain that affirmative action has proved to be of more benefit to black women than black men. Black women, they assert, are more desirable to corporate America because they qualify as two minorities. And, they opine, the white men who do most of the hiring seem to feel more comfortable with black women than they do with the more "threatening" black male.

Complicating matters still further, according to the U.S. Census Bureau, there is an imbalance in the number of black men and women of "marriageable" age [18 and above]. In 1990, there were 11 million black women aged 18 or older. Black men in this age range numbered only 9.3 million. Some of this can be explained by the low life expectancy of black men due to homicide rates, the disproportionate impact of AIDS related illnesses on black males, and war casualties. On average, black women live eight years longer—73 years as compared to 64.9 years—than black men. The remainder of the male/female imbalance, however, is likely attributable to the undercounting of black men by the Census Bureau; most notably men who are part of the underground economy or who reside with a family that is receiving public aid.

Homosexuality, bisexuality and dating or marrying white are prevalent among the most often mentioned factors impacting black male\female relationships. And while lay African Americans fiercely debate these topics, their significance to the Uncivil War are largely discounted by experts. There is little scientific documentation as to extent of homosexuality among black men and women. There is also no hard evidence suggesting that it is more prevalent among women than men, or vice versa. As a result, it can be assumed that the negative impact on the availability of black men caused by homosexuality is roughly offset by the number of black women who are lesbians. The impact of dating outside the race is also insignificant. The rate of interracial marriage by African Americans is the lowest of any ethnic group in America. Less than 5 percent of black men and women marry white.

THE GREAT DEPRESSION

MANY AFRICAN AMERICAN EXPERTS BELIEVE THAT THE UNDER-lying factors causing the Uncivil War go well beyond economics and the availability of suitable partners. They believe that the core issue is depression and the resultant self–defeating behavior of African Americans toward themselves and others.

This despondency, they insist, is a direct consequence of the stubborn *persistence* of racism in America.

In the book, *The Black Family,* black sociologist Hank Allen of Calvin Christian College writes, "Perhaps the most difficult obstacle black families' face is not moral, economic, political or organizational, but physiological–cultural." Black psychologists Derek and Darlene Powell Hopson, in their book, *Friends, Lovers, and Soulmates,* submit: "When Blacks internalize the irrational messages of racism, they feel a sense of worthlessness and powerlessness that creates low self–esteem, depression and self–defeating behavior."

Dr. Cornel West, professor of religion at Harvard University, also points to depression and despair as the catalyst to the Uncivil War. "[A] profound sense of psychological depression, personal worthlessness and social despair" has befallen African Americans, Dr. West writes in his towering book, *Race Matters.* "The frightening result is a numbing detachment from others and a self–destructive disposition toward the world. Life without meaning, hope, and love breeds a cold–hearted, mean–spirited outlook that destroys both the individual and others."

Much of the negative behavior exhibited in black relationships fit Dr. West's characterizations of "cold–hearted" and "mean-spirited." Adultery and abandonment of one's spouse and children are indeed cold–hearted, selfish and cruel. Physical and mental abusiveness is indeed mean–spirited behavior. The same can also be said about African Americans making sweeping negative statements about their own sisters and brothers, such as "black men ain't shit," or "black women are bitches," based upon the actions of only a few.

Unfortunately, relationships are not the only place where African Americans are manifesting despair–inspired, self–destructive behavior. Many young black men are convinced that the only chance that they have to succeed is outside the system. As a result, they have turned to lives of crime, drugs and gangs, and are killing each other at an unprecedented rate. Worse, far too many black people are seeking salvation through alcohol and drugs. But the most telling indicator of the state of mind of many African Americans lies in their rate of suicide. "Until the early `70s," writes Dr. West, "black Americans had the lowest suicide rate in the United States. But now young black people lead the nation in the rate of increase in suicides."

The escalating number of suicides among African Americans, the decline of the black family, and the increase in drugs and crime in the black community *all developed after the end of the Civil Rights era.* This is not coincidental. For all of the joy, hope, dreams, and faith that permeated the black community during the heyday of the Civil Rights Movement, on average, black America is now worse off than it was before the movement began.

It did not take most blacks long to realize that, in the prophetic words of Malcolm X, they had been "hoodwinked." They discovered that federal programs that benefitted African Americans could be implemented in one decade and just as quickly dismantled in the next. Nor did they fail to recognize that when the powers that be were against the rulings of the Supreme Court, they could simply replace the entire body with another more to their liking; or that a national mood of conciliation and fairness that existed during one administration could be easily succeeded by overt racism in the next. After black Americans had struggled so hard to climb up to Dr. King's mountain top, America simply erected another mountain.

By the time Ronald Reagan and his conservative coalition had assumed power, Martin and Malcolm were long dead. And liberalism, black America's philosophical ally, if not dead, was critically wounded. For many African Americans, the swift and frightening fall from the euphoric heights of the Civil Rights era to the brutal racism and inhumanity of the '80s, was just too much for the spirit to endure. Despite the positive benefits of affirmative action and minority set–aside programs, despite the growth of the black middle–class and the end of segregation, the black community in this country is in serious trouble. If African Americans aren't depressed, they damn well should be.

A CALL FOR PEACE

IF EVER BLACK MEN AND WOMEN NEED EACH OTHER, THE TIME IS now. The souls of African American adults require the comfort, encouragement and understanding that only they can give to one another. And our children need a healthy environment in which to develop and grow. They need a community of concerned, loving black men and women—not a war zone.

Today, far too many African American children and young adults are growing up without seeing, let alone experiencing, a positive and stable relationship between a black man and woman. Millions of our children are growing up in single parent households without the benefit of the once commonplace "extended family"—the loving group of aunts, uncles, grandparents and neighbors, both male and female, who formed the "village" that raised our children. It will be quite difficult for these young people to develop healthy relationships if they don't know how. Or worse yet, if they have no evidence that healthy, stable relationships are even possible.

There are, of course, African Americans who have been extremely successful at building fruitful and productive interpersonal relationships, but they are, at this point, far too rare. Yet they still can serve as role models for the active Uncivil War combatants. In subsequent chapters, the lessons learned from successful black couples, as well as former Uncivil War combatants who have found peace, will be shared. In addition, eminent black therapists, sociologists and theologians will give their counsel in an effort to provide more answers, encouragement, and the resources necessary to empower black men and women to find and sustain peace. The Uncivil War must end. But a truce can only be called one black man and woman at a time.

CHAPTER TWO

SELF-INFLICTED
BATTLE WOUNDS

F OR MOST OF THE FOUR HUNDRED–PLUS YEARS THAT
people of African descent have been in America, their
survival in the midst of extreme cruelty and cultural
deprivation has been assured largely as the result of a
strong, stable and supportive black family structure. In the not
too distant past, black men and women understood the obstacles that they faced, and they knew that in order to succeed,
they would have to face them together. They further understood
that the relationship between the black man and woman was
probably—with the possible exception of the black church
—the only aspect of black life that was not acutely influenced
by the long and often oppressive arm of white society.

Today, however, the same harsh economic, cultural and societal forces that once brought black men and women closer
together have evolved to form a wedge that effectually pushes
them apart. From growing despair and hopelessness, to a
widening economic divergence between black women and
black men, to the consistent negative portrayals of black men
and women in the mainstream media, the negative influence of
these powerful external forces are now perilously seeping into
the bedrooms of black America.

It does not have to be this way, however. External pressures
don't cause war; they can only encourage its inception and continuance. External forces also don't wage the battles of the

Uncivil War; individual black men and women do. And it is their thoughts, behaviors, beliefs and attitudes toward the opposite sex that are ultimately the impetus of it all. Consequently, in an effort to better understand the *internal* factors that drive the conflict, in this chapter, we will discuss how images of African Americans are shaped by the media and subsequently influence our behavior. We will also examine what individual black men and women think, say and do to each other that drives them apart, and that then pits them so vehemently against each other.

MYTHS, LIES AND STEREOTYPES

IN CHAPTER 1, WE RECOUNTED HOW THE UNCIVIL WAR IS BEING played out in the media. These televised battles, along with other consistently negative portrayals and images of African Americans, are shaping not only our images of the opposite sex, but of ourselves as well. And not for the better. "...The things that keep black women and black men apart," says Rutgers University professor of psychology Nancy Boyd Franklin, "are partly external but are also partly our own internalization of negative, victimizing messages about each other that have been laid upon us by a Eurocentric society."

Through literature, and the printed and electronic media, America has historically demeaned black intelligence, morals and physical attributes. In place of reality, white America, or what Dr. West calls "white supremacist ideology," has presented negative, stereotypical images of African Americans and their culture. Black men are often portrayed as big, dumb, surly brutes; dangerous men, who are rapists or physically abusive, with incorrigible criminal minds. By the same token, black women are projected as devious, promiscuous Jezebels, prostitutes, or welfare mothers with a house full of dependent children.

The systematic negative portrayal of blacks is older than America herself. Since the mid–fourteenth century, European society has depicted people of African descent as uncivilized, savage heathens. This distorted representation, of course, helped to justify slavery and colonization. The Europeans told themselves they were not exploiting Africans and the resources of Africa, but they were bringing Christianity and civilization to the "Dark Continent."

What is most interesting about European depictions of people of African descent is that prior to the slave trade and the wholesale takeover of Africa by the British, Portuguese and the French, the portrayals of Africans found in European literature, texts, and art were overwhelmingly positive. Dutch scholar Jan Nederveen Pieterse, senior lecturer at the Hague, wrote that in European literature, "the oldest representations of black Africans" were realistic and positive. European portrayals of blacks in ancient Egypt, Pieterse writes in his groundbreaking book, *White on Black*, indicate that black beauty was highly valued in Egyptian culture, and show that blacks were "well integrated into society and intermarrying."

"In the Old Testament," Pieterse continues, "black African kingdoms such as Kush (Saba may also belong in this category) are described as powerful and prestigious..." Throughout Europe, statues of black saints began appearing in the centuries following the death of Christ. St. Augustine (354–430 A.D.), one of the Catholic church's most revered saints, was a black man. In 1300 AD, Pieterse writes, Ethiopians could be found described in European literature as the "beloved Christians of Nubia." And Caspar, the elegant black king of the Moors, became a cult figure in Europe. He was lavishly depicted in Christian literature as one of the Three Kings to attend the birth of Jesus, he was the "public's darling in religous drama" and he was even made the "patron saint of the tailors guild."

By the time European settlers brought Africans to America as slaves, "superior condescension," of African character and culture, writes Pieterse, had "become the tone which predominated in European discourse."

That tone has continued unabated to this day. In his book, The *Assassination of the Black Male Image*, Dr. Earl Ofari

Hutchinson describes a number of attempts by prominent white officials to promote negative myths about African Americans. Dr. Hutchinson cites an *Atlantic Monthly* article published in 1901. In it former U.S. President Woodrow Wilson described African Americans as a "host of dusky children...insolent and aggressive, sick of work, covetous of pleasure." Hutchinson also quotes Dr. G. Stanley Hall, president of the American Psychological Association and founder of the *American Journal of Psychology*. Dr. Hall described African Americans as "erethic, volatile, changeable, prone to transcoidal, intensely emotional, and even epileptoid states." In layman's terms, Dr. Hall had diagnosed African Americans as dangerously unpredictable, irrational and mentally dysfunctional.

More recently, virtually every major newspaper and news magazine in the country has presented stories about a new book that claims blacks are genetically less intelligent than whites. *Newsweek* magazine even used the book, *The Bell Curve* by Charles Murray, for a cover story. The fact that many eminent scientists had found Murray's analysis seriously flawed—for this book as well as his previous one, *Losing Ground*—did not prevent the media from publicizing this recurring stereotype.

In addition to negative depictions of black intelligence and behavior, white America has also vilified the black body. Our eyes and skin were too dark, our noses too flat, our lips and hips too large and our hair too kinky. Throughout American history, African ancestral features have been distorted, caricaturized and otherwise demeaned. At the same time, though, the blonde–haired, blue–eyed white woman became the standard of beauty, and was rendered goddess status in advertisements, magazines, movies and television programs. It was all but impossible for a black child to find a positive representation of the beauty of African Americans in the media. As a result, Dr. Davis points out, studies have confirmed that a significant number of black children prefer playing with white dolls as compared with black ones.

In today's politically correct climate negative images of blacks are, for the most part, subtly presented. These subtle presentations, as well as glaring *omissions*, can be found regularly in major newspapers and television news programs which are far more preoccupied with black failure than black achievement. Contrast, for example, the amount of coverage given to the aftermath of civil war in Rwanda to the *lack* of media attention devoted to one of the most historic events of the twentieth century: the ongoing peaceful transistion of power from white to black in South Africa. Or, compare the number of news stories concerning blacks on welfare and neglected black children to the number of stories about black nuclear families and successful middle–class black couples. Note the emphasis on news stories concerning black crime as compared to the paucity of information on black benevolence and community service.

Black journalist Kirk A. Johnson did some research on media coverage of African Americans to see if the empirical data supported our impressions. The results of his comparative study, published in the *Columbia Journalism Review* and the book, *Unreliable Sources*, were, unfortunately, not surprising. For a one month period, Johnson monitered news stories about Boston's two predominately black neighborhoods. His study included the news reports of six of the largest news media in Boston—two radio stations, three televsion networks, and two daily papers. Johnson found that 85 percent of the news stories concerning the two black neighborhoods "reinforced negative stereotypes of blacks. Blacks," Johnson concluded, "were persistently shown as drug pushers and users, as thieves, as troublemakers, and as victims and perpetrators of violence."

The consistently negative depictions of African Americans is in part a cunning maneuver to keep the attention of whites diverted from their own troubles. Making blacks the scapegoat for America's myriad problems also keeps disparate and potentially antagonistic groups united in preserving the political and economic status quo. In his book, *Tales of a New America*, Clinton Administration Labor Secretary Robert Reich writes about the core parables or myths that most Americans believe in. One of these parables is the "Mob at the Gates." This parable suggests that if Americans are not diligent some evil—Cuba, Iraq, Mexican immigrants, blacks, liberals, atheists, etc.—will destroy the American way of life. In the past the "mob" has included "savage" Indians; Irish, Italian, Slavic and Chinese (the yellow peril) immigrants; Jews and Negroes.

According to Reich, this myth works to preserve economic and political stability by establishing a common destiny and collective identity, primarily for American whites. Unfortunately, this communal spirit ("us") is derived at the expense of other groups ("them").

Reagan and his conservative supporters, Dr. Reich points out, "substantially reconfigured" the Mob at the Gates parable to accomplish their self–serving agenda. This reconfiguration was accomplished through what Dr. Reich calls the "vehicles of public myth": news media, movies, popular fiction, judicial opinions, political speeches and sermons. To justify cuts in social programs, "them" became black welfare queens, "tax and spend" liberals, and big government. To justify increased spending on internal control and defense weaponry, "them" became black rapists and drug dealers, the "Evil Empire" and Middle East terrorists. For added measure, homosexuals, feminists and unions were also thrown into the "them" category.

Fifteen years after the conservatives put their spin on the American parables, the public mindset is vastly changed. Liberalism is a dirty word, government programs are universally considered a failure, movements for equal rights for people of color and women are treading water at best, affirmative action is now called "reverse discrimination" by many, and the ubiquitous violent and dangerous black man has people calling for more jails and longer jail terms.

Impact of Mythology on African American Relationships

FEW AFRICAN AMERICANS WOULD ARGUE ABOUT THE DEGREE to which America negatively distorts the reality of black life.

What would surprise them, however, is the extent to which African Americans themselves buy into the propaganda. They might also be astonished at how much these negative images impact their self–esteem and their relationships with other African Americans.

The consistent lack of positive black images is psychologically devastating to African Americans. "[The] demythologizing of black sexuality is crucial for black America," writes Dr. West, "because so much of black self–hatred and self–contempt has to do with the refusal of many black Americans to love their own black bodies... Just as many white Americans view black sexuality with disgust, so do many black Americans—but for very different reasons and with very different results."

And if a black man or woman has contempt for themselves because they are black, how can they love and cherish another African American? In fact, in many of the interviews with single and married black men and women conducted for this book, negative myths and stereotypes abounded. When speaking of black women, some black men espoused the following opinions about them: "'[Black] women keep scorecards, and measure your assets and job titles'; 'They don't allow us to be ourselves, they want to remake us'; 'Today, a lot of black women are going for white men'; 'I think the white man is still in control of the black woman, and that makes her reject black men'; 'Black women don't respect brothers unless they live up to the materialistic image of a man put out by white society'; 'It's sad that some of our sisters...will do anything for money and fame'; 'Black women are like elephants, they don't forget shit. They will dog you out for something another brother did to them five years ago.'"

Black women also have their strongly held beliefs about black men. Some of these include: "...'There are no good black men available'; 'So many brothers are unemployed because they are lazy'; 'The shortage of black men has made them think of themselves as a prize'; 'All black men want is one thing';

`Black men, in general, are extremely sexist'; 'Too many brothers have no ambition'; 'Black men are cheap'; 'A brother will drop a sister for a white woman in a second.'"

The irony of these stereotypical images held by so many black people about their own folks is that African Americans have been fighting against such nefarious ideas since day one in America. And not just the ones planted by white people. Often demeaning perceptions of blacks have been perpetrated by other blacks. Since the days of slavery, Spelman College President Dr. Johnnetta B. Cole writes in her book, *Conversations,* black men have suggested that "...African American women were in cahoots with White men to degrade African American men. Today, in many Black communities, this most cruel of myths is still being perpetuated, albeit modernized, updated, new and improved."

Unfortunately, far too many black men and women these days find it exceedingly difficult to love or respect their brothers and sisters—or themselves for that matter. And without mutual respect, what chance do we have? "Can genuine human relationships flourish for black people," asks Dr. West, "in a society that assaults black intelligence, black moral character and black possibility?"

THE DECLINE
OF BLACK PRAGMATISM

IN ADDITION TO HOLDING SLANTED BELIEFS ABOUT ONE ANOTHER's worth as a potential partner, many African Americans have distinct and rigid ideas about the roles of men and women in relationships. These concepts basically mirror those of the larger white society. Black expectations of the status and function of a relationship partner are based on the traditional, paternalistic white norms where the husband works and "brings home the bread," while the woman maintains the home and cares for the children. But to base black relationships on white norms, when most African Americans do not have white mind–sets or resources, is unwise.

"I see a lot of [black] couples who have a clash of messages," says Dr. Franklin. They wonder, 'How are we supposed to do this? Are we supposed to do this like the white folks do it? Are we supposed to do it like on the Cosby Show? Are we supposed to do it like our mothers and fathers?' I mean none of this seems to fit. The model of relationships is, for some of our folks, non-existent. They have modeled themselves on the mainstream that doesn't work."

In the past, relationship norms in the black community reflected the realities of black family life. Often professional black women married blue–collar men without regard for who earned the most money or had the best education. Most African American women—unlike their white counterparts—have always worked outside the home, after Emancipation as well as during slavery. Because of the racial barriers that prevented black men from earning sufficient wages to support their families, a large percentage of black women pitched in and helped.

While white mothers were raising their boys to be assertive, many black mothers tried to rear their male children to be passive. Black mothers know that even the slightest public display of aggression or anger by a black male of any age toward a white person could lead to arrest, jail, a beating or worse.

Traditional African society is imbued with a reverence for the spiritual and African American spirituality has been our saving grace in the U.S. For the black community, the church has been the locus not only of worship, but a place that supported traditional culture and values and produced leadership for the struggle for equality. It was also an integral part of the extended black family. In the African tradition, church members comprised part of the "village" of friends, neighbors, and relatives who assisted black parents in rearing their children. The extended family, interestingly enough, was branded dysfunctional by many white sociologists. To them, it was not only foreign, but also contrary to the individualistic, Eurocentric viewpoint which stresses every man and every family for themselves.

Today, African Americans desperately need to define their own relationship norms as they did in the past. Instead, however, many black men expect career–oriented black women, who more and more are ascending to powerful, decision–making positions in all aspects of American society to be demure, darker–skinned versions of "Susie homemaker" after hours. These black men, who some would call sexist, believe that a woman's job is to attend to the needs of her man and the home. They often resent their female partners' efforts to further her career or otherwise improve herself, and they have difficulty with her ability or desire to make decisions—even when the decisions are about how her own hard–earned money will be spent.

In *Black and Single*, Dr. Davis interviewed a professional black man named Arthur who admitted that he gets "a little upset at times by [the] take–charge attitude" of his mate, a professional black woman. "I'm like most black men," says Arthur, "in that I'm in a serious struggle to obtain personal and professional respect from society at large. Everything I see around me tells me that as a man I am supposed to be the chief bread–winner and decision–maker in relationships."

Arthur's acceptance of a Eurocentric definition for his manhood does not reflect the reality of his or other black relations. In 30 percent of married black households, the wives earn more than their husbands. "Black men must understand," writes Dr. Davis, "that romantic relationships, like most other relationships, follow the second Golden Rule: 'He (or she) who has the gold makes the rule....'" Put more broadly, capable black women expect, and rightly so, their knowledge and experience to be respected and valued in their relationships.

Similarly, many black women use individualistic achievement—the Eurocentric standard—as their primary measure of manhood. African–American women, suggest black psychotherapist Derethia Du Val, are looking for black men who fit the white American woman's ideal. "Black women today look for men with the same education, same background and same social standards that they have achieved—and they bypass blue collar workers as possible mates. They are not finding men who match these standards, so they are angry."

Today, many black women, as well as some black men, says Dr. Du Val, believe that the "American dream is obtainable in its white form, not in the black form in which we used to obtain it and were quite comfortable with." Dr. Du Val sees a danger in African Americans allowing "a white mentality or global mentality of the world to keep us from seeking out and searching out our own reality." It is understood by the larger society and needs to be understood by African Americans, she contends, that "a person who *defines himself* cannot be stopped."

Coco, a black woman interviewed in a book on black relationships, *Love Awaits,* agrees with Dr. Du Val assessment. "There aren't enough women who are willing to accept the average, hard-working brother," declares Coco. "We need to realize that we've been taught to expect a myth. And the woman can be the most ordinary, minimum wage–earning, most average–looking woman around, yet she'll insist on having a prince who's earning top dollar. And don't let the sister go to college and have a little bit of education. Then he has to have a doctorate."

Too many black women, as Dr. Du Val and Coco so eloquently points out, are using Eurocentric values as the yardstick to evaluate black men. These values, however, do not take into account the tremendous odds that the average black man, or black woman for that matter, has to overcome to achieve even a modest amount of success in America. Today, black men are still considered a threat to white society, especially by white males. It is more difficult for a black man to stay out of jail than to go to college or aspire to a professional career in corporate America than it is for a black woman. With more and more manufacturing jobs going overseas, black women with basic clerical skills are also finding it easier to get work than non–professional black men.

Furthermore, using individualistic material achievement as a primary indicator of a person's worth ignores the value of a person's contribution to the good of the community which has long been an indispensable part of African American culture. For example, employing a Eurocentric standard, one could equate the business success of the late black multi–millionaire Reginald Lewis, CEO of TLC Beatrice Holdings, Inc. with the much less financially rewarding, but more socially significant achievements of the immortal Rev. Dr. Martin Luther King, Jr. Using an Afrocentric standard to measure the achievements of these two successful black men, Lewis's accomplishments do not even come close to those of Dr. King.

Experts on African heritage and culture have long emphasized that the differences separating black and white Americans go far beyond mere skin color. Meanwhile, Dr. W.E.B. Dubois makes a case for the uniqueness of black culture in his 1903 classic, *The Souls of Black Folks:*

"We the darker ones come even now not altogether empty handed: there are today no truer exponents of the pure human spirit of the Declaration of Independence than the American Negroes; there is no true American music but the wild sweet melodies of the negro slave; the American fairy tale and folklore are Indian and African; and, all in all, we black men seem the sole oasis of simple faith and reverence in a dusty desert of dollars and smartness. Will America be poorer if she replaces her brutal, dyspeptic blundering with light–hearted but determined Negro humility?"

Note Dubois' contrast of white values of "dollars and smartness" with black values of "faith and reverence." Black psychologist Thomas A. Parham also points out that there are major differences in Eurocentric and Afrocentric orientations. Parham writes that the white culture stresses individualism and materialism ["dollars"], rationalization and emotional suppression ["smartness"] and dominance and control ["brutal dyspeptic blundering"]. To the contrary, African American culture, according to Parham, stresses a holistic outlook of spirituality and intuitiveness ["faith"], collective work, community and harmony with nature and other human beings ["humility and reverence"].

Dr. Parham contends that wholesale abandonment of Afro-centric values for Eurocentric ones by African Americans not only negatively impacts black relationships, but also the mental and emotional health of individual African Americans as well. "It is my belief," writes Dr. Parham in his book, *Psychological Storms*," that the degree of psychological and even behavioral devastation one experiences will correspond to the degree of inclusion of Eurocentric values into ones' life. If your sense of self is devoid of spirituality, if your contribution is only to self and not others, if you only compete and never cooperate...and if your sense of worth is externally derived and based upon material wealth rather than self–knowledge and community uplift, then your personal incongruence will be substantial."

ANGER AND VICTIMIZATION

STRONGLY HELD NEGATIVE BELIEFS ARE CRUCIAL TO ANY WAR, and the Uncivil War is no exception. With negative stereotypes comes the ability to easily place the blame for one's own situation onto another party. The South blamed the North, Hitler blamed the Jews and Reagan blamed African Americans and the "Evil Empire" for the problems of the modern world. Woefully, for many African Americans, blaming "bad" black men and women for their own relationship hurts and disappointments has become practically the norm.

If there weren't the option of blaming someone else, there would, in fact, be no war. Of course there would still be unsatisfactory relationships and unfulfilled expectations, but without the ability to shift responsibility, these disappointments would just as likely lead to inner reflection and personal growth as they would to hostility. Instead, however, more and more African Americans count themselves as innocent victims of the opposite sex. And with victimization comes not only powerlessness, but also anger and hostility.

For the men and women who consider themselves martyrs of the Uncivil War, anger has become their battle armor. It protects them from openly and honestly feeling and expressing the hurt of betrayal, the pain of unfulfilled expectations and dreams and the grief of love lost. The victims wear their armor wherever they go, and especially when members of the opposite sex are present. Like a medal of honor, this anger is clearly visible. It can be seen and heard in their body language, their eyes, negative comments and tone of voice.

Commingled with the natural desire to be part of a loving, committed relationship, such ire leads to a strange and unfortunate paradox: Few emotionally healthy people want to spend their valuable, quality time with someone who radiates hostility toward them. As a result, the angry person concludes that their difficulty in meeting and attracting new people is confirmation of their own negative perceptions of the opposite sex, when in reality it is their repugnant anger that is more likely the cause of their troubles.

When an angry black man or woman enters into a new relationship, they often do so consumed with skepticism and acrimony. This, of course, greatly increases the likelihood that the relationship will fail. And again, the blame for the relationship's demise will be undoubtedly assigned to the "enemy," or the opposite sex. Consequently, this same man or woman will drag even more pessimism and hostility into their next relationship, with it, too, doomed to fail. The vicious cycle continues.

WHY NOT A NICE GUY?

STILL ANOTHER OFTEN–CITED FACTOR THAT SPURS THE CONtinuance of the Uncivil War is the frequent selection of inappropriate relationship partners. Many African Americans will relate their goals and desires as being one thing—such as finding a compatible mate who is interested in a committed, long–term relationship—yet they enter into involvements for other, often contrary reasons. These include, but are by no means limited to: Excitement, physical and/or sexual attraction and material gain. Once deeper into the relationship, however, in order to have their desires met, they are forced to try and change the other person or to end the liaison entirely (often bitterly), because their desires went unfulfilled.

In *Friends, Lovers and Soulmates*, the Hopsons talk frankly about the many black men and women they have counseled who repeatedly choose unsuitable relationship partners: "Some women repeatedly become involved with men who physically abuse them. Others may hook up with someone they think they can change. Some men seek out women who will care for them as their mothers did, while others pair up with partners who try to strip them of their self–esteem."

These same types of patterns were consistent with some of those interviewed here. John, the investment banker, claimed that because of the stress of his occupation, he desired a calm and stable relationship. A quiet dinner with stimulating conversation, at home or at an intimate restaurant to John was the perfect romantic evening. As the interview progressed, however, he confided that he was attracted to beautiful, gregarious and "slightly psychotic" women who liked to party and often "hated it" when he wanted to stay home and relax. He then complained that his romantic partners tended to increase the level of stress in his life.

As with John, some black women who profess to desire a stable, committed relationship seem drawn to the men least likely to afford them the opportunity. In an article in Chicago–based *Being Single* magazine, entitled, "Nice Guys: What They Do Wrong," a number of single black women were asked why they refused to date nice guys. The womens' responses included: "'Nice guys try too hard'; 'They put you on a pedestal'; 'A man should have stealth'; 'They have a tendency to be too agreeable or not disagreeable enough' and 'Every little wish becomes their command.'"

According to the article's author, M.K. Allison, many of these same women are purportedly searching for "love and companionship." Unfortunately, Allison concludes, "most routinely pass over the very guys who exemplify what they claim they dream about in a mate."

Dr. Franklin sees the same dynamic at work with some of the

black women she counsels. "A lot of younger women are despairing of ever having the chance to have relationships, says Dr. Franklin, "but I find they sometime overlook the men who are in their lives, men who don't fit the image they have in mind for a mate, or men who lack the chemistry or glitz they are looking for. I ask them to think about the nice man that's been a friend for 20 years who they've never given a chance because he's short or works for the sanitation department or lives with his mother. And what about the man who does their hair, or the man who they call when they need help around the house or with their cars?"

DEFEATING THE ENEMY WITHIN

MANY OF THE WOUNDS SUFFERED IN THE UNCIVIL WAR ARE self–inflicted. Some black men and women, confused by the persistence of negative portrayals of black character, or by unresolved emotional issues, look for and expect the worst in their relationships. And, of course, people usually find what they are looking for.

If a person is serious about "changing their luck" with the opposite sex, they would spend some time on *self–examination*. If relationships consistently fail, the other person can't *always* be blamed. As Dr. Mari Saunders, staff psychologist for the Urban League in Brooklyn, puts it: "The answer is within self. It always is."

CHAPTER THREE

THE PAST AS PROLOGUE

THERE ARE MANY AMERICAN WHITES, AND EVEN some blacks, who want to dismiss the horrific past of blacks in this country. It's as though they believe blacks recently "migrated" to America impoverished and undereducated. The history of blacks in America, however, cannot be discounted. The research and writings of black and white historians and social scientists, including Herbert Aptheker, Lerone Bennett, Andrew Billingsley, W.E.B. DuBois, John Hope Franklin, Paula Giddings, Andrew Hacker, Carter G. Woodson and many others, have carefully documented the truth of African American history and social conditions, past and present. To assign all responsibility for present conditions to the victims of hundreds of years of bondage, Jim Crow and institutionalized and systemic racial bias, is to deny not only this country's past, but also to deny the powerful impact of these combined forces on the lives of black men and women.

In looking at contemporary African Americans, one has to examine how white America dealt with black men, women and their offspring not only during slavery, but in the century following emancipation. Two key legacies of slavery—institutional racism and segregation—have been the critical contributors to keeping a large number of blacks trapped in the lowest strata of American economic, political and social life.

SLAVERY

AFRICAN WOMEN AND MEN FIRST ARRIVED IN THE NORTH American colonies in the early 1600s. Emerging from unspeakably filthy holds of slave ships, they were shackled in chains to prevent their escape from the traders who had transported them from Africa to provide labor for the colonists. Strangers in a new world, the Africans were also strangers to each other, having come from diverse African tribes, mostly on that continent's West Coast. The Africans had no choice but to improvise a new language by combining the languages they knew with the European languages being spoken to them. They also had to devise ways to survive the humiliation of long, hard, unpaid labor for their captors, brutal physical punishment, degradation, deprivation and a radically different social and material climate.

Slaves were considered chattel, treated as property, not as men and women with human feelings and human rights. Their capture in Africa, horrendous passage across the Atlantic Ocean and dispersal in the colonies, seriously contorted their social structures and family units. As slaves, Africans were allowed familial bonds only at the discretion of the slave owner. What is laudable is that the Africans were wonderfully creative and able to develop viable new social structures and family relationships within the institution of slavery.

Family Life in Bondage

THE ANCIENT PATTERNS OF AFRICAN COURTSHIP, MARRIAGE and family life that the newly captured Africans had known were disallowed under slavery. Blacks were forbidden to speak their own languages. Nor could they practice their traditional religions and rituals or follow any of the customs that were a part of their lives before the brutal Middle Passage. But mating between males and females is instinctual and black men and women came together as couples within the constraints of their bondage even though both were considered the property of their owners, as were their children. Some slaveholders also recognized that familial relationships had a stabilizing influence on their plantations. Consequently, courtships and slave marriages were allowed to take place throughout much of the South, where the majority of enslaved blacks lived.

Because legally documented marriage between slaves was not allowed, blacks sealed their unions by jumping over a broomstick. Festive plantation weddings were sometimes officiated by white ministers, although most often black preachers presided over the ceremony. The vows that slave couples exchanged were honored by the couple and other slaves and, to some degree, by the slave owner. If both newlyweds lived on the same plantation, they were often allowed to have their own space in the slave quarters. The husband could hunt for game and catch fish to supplement the inadequate diet that the slaveholder provided. After working in the fields or in the owner's house, the wife would cook, clean, mend clothes and perform other domestic chores for her own family. Black men, as far as possible, fulfilled the traditional male role as head of the family and their wives and children treated them with respect.

Unfortunately, the fact was that black males could not protect their mates, mothers, sisters or daughters from sexual exploitation and other cruelties of slavery. Black men who tried to protect black women, or to express anger at their maltreatment, were savagely beaten, if they were not killed outright. It was essential to the slavemaster's control that the men they held captive be constantly made aware of their powerlessness, and sexual exploitation of black women was the primary method used as a reminder. As DuBois said several years later, "…White men want the right to use all women, colored and white, and they resent the intrusion of colored men in this domain."

EMANCIPATION

SLAVERY ENDED IN AMERICA WHEN THE UNION ARMY DEFEATed the Confederacy in the Civil War, bringing emancipation to four million slaves. Another nearly half million free Negroes were split between the Confederate states and the Northern states that had ended slavery between 1777 and 1804.

Freedom wasn't all that the former slaves expected it to be. The redistribution of land that had been confiscated by the Union was largely a farce. Freedmen in some states were given the poorest, least attractive acreage and no support to develop it. (Ironically, in the next century some of this land proved quite valuable.) Other freed slaves seized plantation lands that had been abandoned by defeated Confederates. A great number of freedmen, however, found themselves without a home or work and unable to take care of themselves and their families. Just as it had been during slavery, many black men could not provide for or protect their women and children.

(During the Civil War, General William Sherman had promised some blacks up to 40 acres of land. The promise was never fulfilled, but neither was it forgotten. Film director Spike Lee's production company is called 40 Acres and a Mule. And in 1994 black activists raised the issue in the national media of reparations for all blacks for their unpaid slave labor.)

RECONSTRUCTION

THERE WERE SOME POSITIVES FOR FAMILIES DURING RECON- struction. Many former slaves had the chance to reunite with kin who had escaped or been sold off their plantations during slavery. Couples who had "jumped the broom" took advantage of new laws that allowed them to legalize their marriages. Thousands of men and women traveled north and west to find loved ones. Often, they placed advertisements in the press to help them in their search. The October 14, 1865 edition of the *Colored Tennessean* newspaper carried one such ad. Benjamin and Flora East offered to pay $100 each for information about their son or daughter who had been sold away from them in Nashville, traced to Mississippi, then to Texas. There was great joy when family members were reunited.

This joy, however, was often shortlived as blacks began to face the realities of their new freedom. Former slaveholders, with a distinct aversion to paying for the labor they had enjoyed for free for hundreds of years, and harboring a fear that former slaves would exact revenge for past injustices, devised a scheme that effectively continued the servitude and powerlessness of blacks.

Sharecropping was the answer to any would-be slaveholder's fondest dreams. The system of sharecropping was actually tenant farming where the landowner had all the advantages. The landowner allowed a landless farmer to occupy a small portion of his land. The tenant farmers, both black and white, worked the land raising cash crops and doing some gardening for food. To obtain the seeds and equipment required to produce the crops, the tenant farmer often had to borrow money, usually from the landowner. The tenant farmer's indebtedness accumulated not only from borrowing to work the land, but also because the major portion of his crop belonged to the landowner. Whatever the sharecroppers could earn from selling their portion of the crop was, more often than not, completely offset by their debts. Being in debt to the landowner at the end of each season meant they had to remain where they were and make yet another futile effort to save enough money to move away or buy their own land.

Although tenant farming did provide some blacks with a way to minimally care for their families, it was a tough and unfair life. Corrupt landowners managed the system so that the largely illiterate sharecroppers either never broke even, or made minimal profits. Every member of the family—husbands, wives and children of all ages—worked long, hard hours just to subsist.

White Resistance

MOST WHITES, ESPECIALLY THOSE WITH LOW INCOMES AND little education, feared blacks would take land, housing and employment away from them. Having always been told that blacks were inferior beings, these whites felt betrayed by the 13th, 14th and 15th amendments to the Constitution. These amendments were passed by Congress in 1865, 1866 and 1870, respectively, to guarantee civil and voting rights and to permanently outlaw slavery. These largely powerless whites emphatically did not want to compete with blacks for their livelihoods.

Defeated Southerners put into place a system of discrimination in jobs, education, housing and voting (the infamous Jim Crow laws) designed to keep black men and women in subservient positions. Blacks had limited options: they could submit, become entrepreneurs and develop their own institutions, or leave the South. Blacks struggled to better their lives through hard work and education. Southern white men on the other hand, organized a social club in Pulaski, Tennessee in 1865 and spread terror across the South during and after Reconstruction. The club, named the Ku Klux Klan, lynched, beat, and killed black males and burned their homes seemingly without restraint. When they did not commit violence, they used intimidation and threats of violence. Congress enacted a series of "Force Laws" beginning in 1870 to curb the Klan, but they had little effect.

Women hired themselves out to do the same domestic chores they had done when they were enslaved and men continued to do the back-breaking labor for low wages that they had previously done for no pay. Some men were adamant about not exposing their women to the continuing threat of sexual exploitation by whites and refused to allow them to work as domestics away from home. Many of these women developed "cottage industries" as seamstresses and laundresses in their own homes. Madame C.J. Walker, before she founded a million dollar hair care business, was self-employed as a laundress for nearly 20 years.

Many black men who were able and willing to be away from home for extended periods found work in the expanding national railway system as sleeping car porters, cooks and maintenance crew. Steady money allowed them to house, clothe and feed their families. Steady work gave them a sense of pride and confidence. As head of their households black men worked long hours, sometimes at more than one job, to earn enough to have their wives stay at home and care for their children. Blacks were often part of extended families that included parents, grandparents, aunts, uncles, cousins and friends who were "like family." Neighbors also helped each other in informal mutual-aid networks. All of these people provided emotional and physical support for the couple, giving them the benefit of their combined experience.

THE GREAT MIGRATION

AS THE NINETEENTH CENTURY DREW TO A CLOSE, A NUMBER OF blacks began to migrate out of the South, away from the unrelenting oppression. They moved to the West, Midwest and North in search of better opportunities. The migration was generated by the hope of finding work in new industries in Cleveland, Chicago, Detroit, Pittsburgh, St. Louis and other large cities. *The Pittsburgh Courier* and *The Chicago Defender* newspapers encouraged blacks to leave the South for the jobs that could be found in other regions. Letters home from those who had already migrated encouraged others to follow.

Between 1880 and 1920, the black population of Chicago increased from 6,480 to 109,458, almost doubling during each decade of this period. Similarly, New York's black population grew from 19,663 to 152,467.

The great migration North, however, presented black men and women with new social and economic obstacles. For one thing, it wasn't always possible for the entire family to move at the same time. Husbands often moved first to find work and a place for the family to live. The separation put emotional as well as physical distance between couples who then communicated primarily by mail. When couples were reunited, there was often a stressful adjustment period. The men were familiar with the faster, more sophisticated city life and the "country" women had to learn to adapt to that life.

The great migration was also the beginning of a change in extended family units as parents and children moved away from grandparents, aunts and uncles. These members of the extended family had not only served as unpaid child caretakers, but were also mediators of disputes and disagreements between married couples.

ROARING TWENTIES AND THE GREAT DEPRESSION

THE BLACK MEN WHO SERVED IN WORLD WAR I WERE STRICTLY segregated at home and overseas. And when they returned home in 1917 they found the same discrimination and racial hatred that existed before the War. Some of the country's worst race riots broke out in Washington, D.C., Chicago and 23 other cities and towns in the spring and summer of 1919, sometimes referred to as "The Red Summer." The Klan lynched scores of blacks throughout the South and were an ever-present threat to black men and their families.

In addition to the Klan, these was also increasing economic difficulties as the demand for labor decreased somewhat after the war. There were, however, still jobs available in some cities in the industrial north in the early 1920s. Black men were hired for back-breaking, but relatively well-paying jobs in Pittsburgh's steel mills, Chicago's meat packing houses, Detroit's automobile plants and New York's garment industry. Black women also found employment as laborers in some of these industries, and as always, as low-paid domestic workers.

Every area of life changed for blacks with the Stock Market Crash of 1929. The country was plunged into a Great Depression and grinding poverty swept across America like a vengeful equalizer. Whites were as poor as blacks, but they maintained their attitude of racial superiority and bigotry continued unabated. Black unemployment was severe. According to government census reports, 25 to 30 percent of the black population—not much different than today—was out of work.

The Depression was so devastating to white America that the U.S. government was forced to establish relief programs for workers and farmers across the country. Dozens of New Deal programs established under President Franklin D. Roosevelt ultimately benefitted blacks. The National Youth Administration, whose Division of Negro Affairs was directed by educator Mary McLeod Bethune, provided jobs for young workers. The Public Works Administration hired skilled and unskilled laborers, and the Farm Security Administration extended loans to indigent farmers and sharecroppers.

Aid to Dependent Children (ADC, now AFDC, Aid to Families with Dependent Children) or welfare, as it came to be called, was also established at this time. According to the guidelines of the program, children could not qualify as truly dependent on government assistance if there were an able-bodied man in the household. To comply with ADC rules men had to absent themselves, or pretend to be absent, from their families. This increased the feelings of emasculation and humiliation already generated by unemployment. The laws undercut the men's role as head of the family and made it difficult for them to assert their authority. Many men felt forced to participate in the charade, however, for the sake of their families' survival, but others left never to return.

THE CIVIL RIGHTS MOVEMENT

THE YEARS FOLLOWING WORLD WAR II PROMISED MORE JOB opportunities for black men and women. More than one million had served in the war which ended in 1945. The Truman Administration instituted a Fair Deal Policy to eliminate segregation in government service, and organizations like the NAACP and Urban League continued their pressure for civil rights. Jobs opened up in the automotive, electronics, chemical and aircraft industries. As a result, the next decade and a half was a period of rising expectations as efforts to end segregation grew into the Civil Rights Movement.

The beginning of the Civil Rights Movement is most often set at the 1954 Supreme Court school desegregation decision. "Integration" became the by-word and black men and women marched and protested side by side with fair-minded whites to end racism. Some areas of conflict between black men and women, however, were highlighted by the structure of the civil rights organizations. Many of the organizations were closely allied to, and modelled after, black churches where men were the leaders. In most churches the pastors and important officers were men while women were assigned to manage auxiliary and support areas.

In Martin Luther King, Jr.'s Southern Christian Leadership Conference, in the NAACP, the Urban league and the Congress of Racial Equality (CORE), black men held the leadership positions that set policy and decided on strategy. The feeling of black men, and some black women, within and outside the organizations was that it was important for men to be in the forefront, to assert themselves as leaders in a manner that emulated the larger, white society. Black men acknowledged the traditional strength of black women, but now they wanted women to take a more subservient role as a supportive, rather than an equal partner.

A Woman's Place

FOR THE MOST PART, BLACK WOMEN IN THE MOVEMENT WERE in agreement for they had been long-time witnesses to the black man's emasculation under racism and segregation. Generally speaking, black women were ready for black men to take the role of "warrior" and stand up to the system in a forceful non-violent way. As a result, a great many of the women in the movement worked happily behind the scenes, wo-manned the offices, cooked meals and kept house for volunteer marchers and Freedom Riders.

There were a number of black women on the front lines, however, singing, demonstrating and going to jail along with the black men. And a few women, like Ella Baker, Fannie Lou Hamer, Septima Clark, and Bernice Reagon gained prominence for their courage and the leadership they gave to the struggle. They were the exceptions, though, rather than the rule.

During the period from 1954 through 1968, black men and women had a *purpose,* a national struggle to attend to. Whether they lived in the North or the South, the struggle demanded that they present a united front. But there were private discussions taking place between black men and women about their roles during this period and later during the push for black power.

Black women who were active in the front lines, especially those who were good theorists or tacticians, resented the fact that they were being pushed back and basically told to be quiet. Although there was no talk then of women's liberation, some women were not as acquiescent as others and wanted to be recognized for their contributions. Black men tried to persuade black women that it was for the good of the race that the men be in the lead. It was another instance of emulating those who were in power. White men had the vast majority of leadership roles in the larger society, so it seemed that to be "equal" black men had to be the leaders of black organizations. There was also an implied promise that when the struggle was over, black women would be allowed to fill larger, more key roles. Perhaps black women didn't want to appear to be fulfilling the myths and stereotypes of the black matriarchy, the castrating, domineering black female. Or maybe, they, too, believed that to be integrated with whites, they needed to *behave the same as whites*. In any case, black women largely submitted to the men's wishes.

There was also another area of uneasiness between black men and black women. A lot of black men in the Civil Rights and Black Power movements considered women as the rewards for soldiers or warriors who were on the front lines. Their idea was that women were mainly present for sex and domestic duties. An oft-repeated quotation that has been attributed to Stokely Carmichael (now Kwame Toure) is that "the best position for women [in the struggle] is prone."

White Women

THAT ATTITUDE ANGERED SOME BLACK WOMEN, BUT THEY AND others were hurt even more when many black men in the 1960s and 1970s turned to white female activists for companionship and sex. Black men explained that they were dating white women as an act of revenge against white men for raping black women during slavery. Even accepting that explanation as true, the battle between black and white men over white women still left black women on the sidelines, *alone*. Not a few black women feel that the black men who slept with white women during the 1960s and 1970s movements were "claiming the prize" that had for so long been forbidden.

Some black women, refusing to be left out, responded favorably to the attention they received from white men in the movement. During this rather unprecedented period of black and white togetherness, many people had their first opportunity to really know a person of the other race. However, the issue of white lovers was a source of contention between black men and women and continues to be a highly emotional and sensitive subject for many.

Differences in Educational Attainment

IN ANY NUMBER OF BLACK FAMILIES WITH MALE AND FEMALE siblings, one or more of the females will obtain a college education. The males in the family, however, tended to go into the armed services, find skilled or unskilled labor, or, if they don't want a regimented life, earn a livelihood with a street "hustle." Unlike their sisters, boys are encouraged to be willful and involved in sports and other "manly" pursuits, or to work part time. Girls, on the other hand, are taught to be disciplined, to study hard and to help out at home. A lot of blacks attribute this pattern to the old saying that black mothers "raise their daughters, but love their sons." However, this difference in educational attainment has a historical base.

Traditionally, black parents knew that their sons could obtain blue collar occupations and earn enough to support themselves and their families. But, more often, their daughters, whose major avenue for employment was domestic work, were sent to college. (Very few expected that their daughters would not work.) As a consequence, black parents encouraged their daughters to be good students because college was the only way for them to avoid "Miss Ann's" kitchen. Their sons, who could earn "good" money in factories and foundries, often dropped out of school early to get a job. This historical adaptation to post–war conditions has evolved into disparate expectations for the education of black boys and girls.

The lowered anticipation of success along with the larger society's ever–present apprehensiveness about black males, have combined to ensure that black boys don't receive the attention or encouragement in school that they should. In the last several years black social scientists and others have begun to describe how black boys are discriminated against in the primary grades. Many black males recall their early school years when their natural energy earned them the label of "problem" students. Others who were inattentive or disinterested in the style of teaching were called slow learners and put into separate classes where even less was expected of them. Those black boys for whom academic attainment is discouraged, both at school and in the community, rarely go on to higher education. Consequently, many black men have been unable to take advantage of the same educational grants and opportunities that black women obtained.

THE WOMEN'S MOVEMENT

THE 1970s SAW OPENINGS FOR BLACKS IN WHITE COLLAR POSI-tions in corporate America that previously had not existed. Additionally, the Women's Liberation Movement created a push to open doors for women in business and as has often been indicated, employers could fulfill both gender and racial quotas by hiring a black woman. Black men also suspected that black women were preferred to them because white employers perceive black women to be less threatening than black men.

Although few black women joined the ranks of demonstrating women's liberationists, many did agree with the call for equality with men. The issue of sexism and male domination raised by white feminists struck a responsive chord in black women causing them to look at their own history with black men. And the truth was that sexism was and always had been a part of their relationships.

By tradition and circumstance black men occupied the dominant role in most black families and organizations and this had largely been accepted by black women. However, the financial independence that came with education and better paying jobs made black women less willing to put up with sexism, or any other type of abuse, from black men. Black women also had more control over their lives with the advent of easier methods of birth control and legalized abortion, which they took advantage of, often over the protests of black men. As Paula Giddings stated in *When and Where I Enter*, "Throughout the social history of black women, children are more important than marriage in determining the woman's domestic role."

Black men did not see themselves as oppressors of their women; rather, they saw themselves as the victims of white America. For the most part, they berated the Women's Liberation Movement as an activity of spoiled white women who wanted to denigrate the same white men who had put them on pedestals. Black women had no place in that movement, black men declared. By and large, black men feel that any problems between black men and women can be worked out by the two of them, without calling on the rhetoric of the women's movement.

Whether influenced by the woman's movement or not, today, black women are vying for the highest positions they can achieve and are challenging men to overcome the same obstacles that women have. Black women know that if they can succeed in school and the work world, so can black men. To many black men this attitude makes black women less desirable as marriage partners. Other women, sympathetic to the black man's plight, agree that his life is more difficult. The issue of who has it easier or tougher has actually become a point of contention between black men and women. In the meantime, however, black women keep moving forward.

While many black men say that they are not intimidated by a woman with more education and/or a higher salary, education and money continue to be sore points between black women and men. Black men say that it is not so much the money or the degree, but the attitude of superiority that these black women bring to the relationship. There are black men, though, who say they welcome the opportunity to date or marry well paid executive women.

Deferring Marriage

IN THE LAST TWENTY-FIVE YEARS THERE HAVE BEEN MAJOR changes on the dating and marriage front for black women and men. Both sexes are marrying later, and both have reservations about marrying at all. Black women, armed with the means to adequately support themselves, set their sights on partners with similar assets and credentials. Many refuse to accept a mate who has any less and so are hesitating to marry at all.

The reluctance to marry is only one factor contributing to the large number of single black folks today. Other factors are the same old, but true, story of hard economic times and the effects of continuing racism. As the 1992 book, *Children of the Dream* by Audrey Edwards and Craig K. Polite, states, "For the African-American, race continues not only to make a critical impact on success and achievement, but also to skew how black success and achievement are viewed: inevitably it is in relation to white success." This feeling that blacks never quite measure up contributes to the plagues of drug and alcohol abuse, homicide, and the high percentage of black prison inmates that decimate the numbers of eligible black men.

PAST AS PROLOGUE

ALTHOUGH THE OBSTACLES OF THE 1990s ARE DIFFERENT FROM those faced by the Africans brought here hundreds of years ago, the same determination to overcome is required to ensure survival. African Americans who are knowledgeable about the history of blacks in America believe that the current situation has its genesis in the events of the past. Things changed dramatically for blacks educationally and financially after the social movements of the 1960s and 1970s, but those years also brought upheavals in traditional black relationships.

Today there seems to be an impasse with many black women and men looking at each other as adversaries rather than partners and friends. It is also apparent, however, that their long history together in this country has created a durable bond that even the worst of times and conditions won't sever.

CHAPTER FOUR

THE UNCIVIL WAR, CONDENSED AND TELEVISED:

CLARENCE THOMAS vs. ANITA HILL

I N THE FIRST WEEK OF OCTOBER 1991, JUDGE CLARENCE Thomas, an appointee of President George Bush to the United States Court of Appeals for the District of Columbia, was all but confirmed by the U.S. Senate Judiciary Committee to take a seat on the U.S. Supreme Court when a megaton bomb was rudely detonated. That bomb was the news—leaked to National Public Radio and New York *Newsday*—that Anita Hill, a black, female law professor and former colleague of Thomas, had given a confidential affidavit to the Senate Judiciary Committee and a report to the FBI that Thomas had sexually harassed her some ten years earlier when she worked with him at the Department of Education and later at the Equal Employment Opportunity Commission (EEOC).

The leak, and the testimony that it prompted, created a furor that not only changed forever the way American men and women look at their interactions, especially in the workplace; but also impacted electoral politics. Hill's sworn allegations brought a dramatic halt to confirmation proceedings that had been winding to a close. A hearing was set to give the Judiciary Committee of fourteen white male senators an opportunity to hear a more complete account of the charges from Hill, and to get a response from Thomas. What they, and a riveted television audience of millions, got was living theater, a political-racial-sexual cliffhanger starring two of America's "best and brightest" blacks, with cameo appearances by their peers and an impressive array of black civil servants. In key supporting roles were various members of the Washington press corps. As the spectacle played out, the cast also included a widening circle of lobbyists for a variety of pressure groups, demonstrators of every stripe, former classmates and colleagues of Hill, then 35, and Thomas, then 43, their family members and neighbors.

From the start, those who were most involved—or touched by the case groped for words to characterize the hearings—"a circus," was one of Thomas's milder appellations; "one of the most painful proceedings in the history of the Congress and the nation...[a] horrendous scene," lamented Congressman Edolphus Towns (D-N.Y.).

Hill's charges threatened Thomas's confirmation in a way that his EEOC record on the aged, his silence on Roe v. Wade and widespread uneasiness about his qualifications to sit on the nation's highest court had not. Once the allegations were published and a hearing scheduled on the Judiciary Committee calendar, impassioned arguments began across the country about what really went on between Hill and Thomas and which one of them was telling the truth. People debated and theorized in their offices, on college campuses, in bars and around the dinner table. It was the main topic of discussion wherever people gathered, from the time of the leak until long after the hearings ended on Monday, October 15.

There was no place, however, where agony and dismay, shock and fury were felt more deeply than in the African American community. All of black America was caught off-guard by the case, trapped in the unrelenting, unblinking glare of an ugly media event. Two successful blacks who should have stood (willing or not) as shining examples of dignity and achievement were instead "washing their dirty linen in public." Black America was acutely embarrassed for Hill, Thomas, and for the community as a whole. Others felt ashamed and degraded at hearing frank references to sex organs and pornography. While the black community has been depicted by whites as morally loose and sexually uninhibited, there is, in fact, a streak of conservatism among many black women and men when it comes to sexual matters. It is rare for blacks to discuss sex at a public gathering and unprecedented for it to be talked about before a mostly white audience of millions. Many were angry that at a time when African Americans faced so many critical social and political issues, that a case of lurid sexual allegations between a black man and woman was the focus of the spotlight.

BLACK COMMUNITY SHARPLY DIVIDED

AS DETAILS OF THE CHARGES AND THE HISTORY OF THOMAS' and Hill's relationship came to light, it was almost impossible for a black adult male or female to remain neutral on the issue. And there was no consensus of opinion among blacks, either. The differences sometimes fell along gender lines and sometimes they didn't. Within the black community, both Thomas and Hill had men and women who rallied behind them and each had critics who damned them. The positions taken by blacks—the side chosen, the speculative conclusions—were quite revealing of the ongoing Uncivil War between black men and black women, and the way they regard each other and themselves.

The battle between Thomas and Hill and the long weekend of hearings was a condensed version of this Uncivil War. Almost all the issues that contribute to that war were on display: the stereotyping of black male sexuality, the input of white feminists, interracial marriage, and particularly the belief that black women should give unquestioning support and loyalty to black men, especially in the face of white opposition.

When the final senate roll call was taken at the end of the hearings, Clarence Thomas was confirmed by one of the lowest margins of this century (53 yeas, 48 nays). Although no one other than he and Hill would ever really know what had occurred between them in 1981 and 1982, more senators than not found him an acceptable choice for the Supreme Court.

At the start of the confirmation hearings, Thomas had the support of over half the country's blacks and an equal proportion of the whites who were polled. By the end of the hearings, the night before the vote, blacks and whites believed him over Hill by a ratio of 2-1. One year later, however, an *U.S. News and World Report* poll showed a sharp shift in opinion, with Americans almost evenly divided on whom they believed. Almost 40 percent of those who were polled thought that Hill had been treated unfairly by the Senate panel and there was a 10 percent drop in those who thought that Thomas should have been confirmed.

Why were so many in the black community increasingly hostile to Anita Hill from the moment her charges were aired until the final senate count?

First and foremost, Hill was perceived as a traitor to one black man and, by extrapolation, to all black men and the community as a whole. From the brutal attempts to emasculate black men during slavery up to contemporary institutional biases that result in a disproportionate number of black men being incarcerated in jails and prisons, African American men have borne the brunt of white racism. It has been the traditional role of black women to support, comfort and encourage black men. It is a role that black women have accepted and fulfilled while expressing little public resistance or resentment until the last couple of decades. One of the main reasons black women accepted the role of comforter so readily was an acknowledgement on their part that the white males who hold the vast majority of power are inordinately threatened by black males. Consequently, black women have generally had an easier time manipulating the system than black men have. Even with the advent of the women's liberation movement, the pattern of black women deferring to black men publicly, if not always in private, has been considered necessary for survival of the family and the race. Black women who openly counter this tradition are often criticized within the community and branded traitors, man-haters, "Sapphires" or lesbians.

THE CONSPIRACY

THERE IS A STRONG TENDENCY WITHIN THE COMMUNITY TO believe that there is a conspiracy by white America to destroy black men. This belief is supported by the grim statistics on the economic, educational and health status of blacks in this country. A further indication of the conspiracy is the number of prominent black men who have been subject to public charges of corruption. According to a report in *GQ* (December 1993) entitled "The Witch Hunt" by Mary A. Fischer, "...of the 465 political-corruption probes initiated between 1983 and 1988, 14 percent targeted black officials, though they made up only 3 percent of all U.S. officeholders....In the [U.S.] House of Representatives, ...roughly half of the then twenty-six members of the Congressional Black Caucus were the target of federal investigations and/or indictments between 1981 and 1993. For the numbers to be equal for white respresentatives, 204 of the 409 white House members would have been subjected to the same scrutiny during that time, yet according to Justice Department figures, only 15 actually were."

In "Sex, Lies & Stereotypes," an *Emerge* (January 1992) magazine article on the Thomas-Hill confrontation written by Sylvester Monroe, he says that in addition to Thomas, Marion Barry and Mike Tyson, Funk singer Rick James, actors Jim Brown and Eddie Murphy, former Illinois Congressman Gus Savage and *Washington Post* journalist Juan Williams have all been accused of sexual misconduct. Taken together, these two journalistic accounts lend credence to the black community's conspiracy theory and to the words of Ray Jarvis, a consultant on race and gender issues in the workplace, who is quoted by Monroe as saying, "Negative news about black men sells, and that's the easiest news to sell about blacks."

Anyone—especially a woman—who is perceived as "putting

the black man down," is thought to be working on the side of the conspirators.

In the Hill-Thomas case, Professor Hill was considered by many to be a tool of the senators, white feminists and other whites who opposed Thomas's (or any other black man's) ascension to the vacant Supreme Court seat. Viewed as a traitor by some, she took her place in a "hall of shame" alongside other black women like Hazel "Rasheeda" Moore, in the Barry case; Desiree Washington, in the charge against Tyson; and the recently added Mary Stansel whose lawsuit precipitated the NAACP's ouster of Benjamin Chavis in 1994.

Hill was vilified for her timing: detractors wondered why she had not taken her complaints to the proper authorities (or to Thomas himself) in 1981 or 1982. In "Public Hearing, Private Pain," a documentary about the case shown on television's *Frontline*, a number of black women who were interviewed suggested that Hill should have maintained her ten-year silence. One Macon, Georgia woman said, "It's best to leave it alone—don't bring up the dirt. Let it stay behind closed doors."

For some, the idea that Hill's charges may have been true made no difference in their opinion that she should not have brought the matter up if she had let so many years pass without revealing it. They asked, "Why do so ten years after the fact, if not to destroy Thomas?"

Initially, Hill received little sympathy for the harassment charge because the concept was a relatively new one for the nation as a whole, and for the black community, in particular. Some black men argued that sexual banter between African American men and women has been a fact of life (as it is between whites, and interracially). Black women also acknowledged that this kind of innuendo from men on the street and at work was such a common occurrence that they had learned to deal with it. When a lone black woman walks past two or three black men who are together, she expects that one or more of them will make a comment, ranging from a simple, "hey, baby," to something about her looks or a part of her anatomy. The woman responds with a greeting or a lecture, ignores the remark, or curses the men out depending on her own sensitivity and self-esteem. But most black women consider raw, crude comments by men on the street to be an insulting act of aggression they would rather not be exposed to.

There's a kind of easy-going, acceptable sexual repartee that takes place between lovers and friends. However, this kind of talk is not considered appropriate between an employer/ supervisor and an employee, casual acquaintances or strangers. Black men usually don't see their sexually suggestive comments as insults. For some, it's their way of paying a woman a compliment. Jennifer Tucker, deputy director of the Center for Women Policy Studies in Washington, D.C. responds to this type of attitude by saying "Black men who know what racism is and experience it often have no idea what sexism is or how it impacts women. The sense of denial is so strong in our community that it is frightening."

Another explanation for behavior that many women consider unwelcome, is that sexual boasting is a part of the culture. Rap music by best-selling male groups specializes in this kind of macho posturing (exemplified by Luke Campbell of 2 Live Crew, aka Captain Dick). All too often, though, rap is coupled with disrespect and/or violence toward females.

Until the Hill-Thomas hearing heightened the country's awareness of how women might feel about sexual references from men who are not their intimates, black women had been relatively quiet about the way they have been spoken to or referred to by black males. Except for occasional books and newspaper columns, there were few public forums for women to express their sensibilities on the issues about black men that disturb them. Media consultant Emily Tynes, who appeared in "Public Hearing, Private Pain" pointed out that while black women have always been called upon to be superwomen— "nurturers, activists, supporters of black men...workhorses who work harder and get paid less"—an unspoken code in the community doesn't allow them "to express or work through the trauma they've experienced."

In an interview in *Essence* magazine (March 1992), Anita Hill herself said, "As African-American women, we are always trained to value our community even at the expense of ourselves....We are constrained from expressing our negative experiences because they are perceived in the larger community, as a bad reflection on African Americans....It's an unfortunate and awful position for Black women to be in. It's interesting that people haven't seen the harassment of Black women as a betrayal."

Anita Hill was an easy target for some of the more imaginative scenarios that were proffered. In the early 1980s, she had been a single black professional woman in Washington, D.C., a city where single professional women greatly outnumber single professional men, repeating a pattern that exists nationwide. The fact that Thomas had indeed been divorced from a black woman, and then dated and wed a white woman only fueled the gossip. After all, the talk went, Hill was angry at having to face the same kind of rejection black women have often faced from black men who prefer white women to black ones.

These were some of the more benign things said about Hill in the weeks after her allegations were made known and mushroomed into the issue of the year. Various reporters and commentators speculated that she was a tool of white political interests including southern segregationists like Senator Strom Thurmond who publicly supported Thomas because he was mindful of his black constituency, but who actually did not want a black justice on the Supreme Court. Others said Hill was being backed by white feminists because they needed a major issue like sexual harassment to pump new life into a movement that was losing strength and visibility.

IS IT RACISM OR SEXISM?

THE FACT THAT SHE SPOKE OUT, THAT SHE BROUGHT UNWANTED attention to the black community cost Anita Hill and her family. "My parents were exposed to ugliness in a way that was really unfair, and unfortunate, and hurtful to them," Hill said a year later. "I was publicly vilified...and that's something that I would not wish on anybody else." In spite of what she called a "reprehensible" response to her speaking out, Hill encouraged other women to come forward whenever they are victims of sexual harassment.

In the three days over which the Judiciary Committee hearing took place, Clarence Thomas also portrayed himself as a victim—a victim of "a high-tech lynching for uppity blacks." By evoking one of the most racially-charged images possible, Thomas shrewdly and dramatically turned the hearing in his favor. Whites and blacks were reminded of the not so distant past when black men swung from trees simply for being black, and especially when it was suspected they had in some way offended a white woman.

There were several ironies in Thomas' cynical use of a shameful (for whites) and painful (for blacks) historical image, not the least of which was his prior insistence that racism had not been a problem for him. A further irony was that Thomas was not being accused by a white woman, but a black one. And the most visible irony of all was that his major support came from whites, specifically Senator John Danforth of Missouri and Thomas' wife, who sat directly behind him.

But Thomas played the race card for all it was worth and it worked. Senators fearful of voting reprisals from black constituents or of being labelled racist, dropped their reservations about him amid an outpouring of sympathy for Thomas from blacks who wanted another black man to replace Justice Thurgood Marshall on the Supreme Court. And once Thomas had his lifetime appointment to the bench, many blacks reasoned, he would surely remember his black roots, his debt to the Civil Rights Movement and affirmative action programs and would vote with an understanding of the plight of oppressed people.

Reaction to the total three-day spectacle and the final vote was tumultuous, emotional, loud, and three years down the road, unending. Feminists adopted Hill as their new national heroine and she was given awards for her "courage," and daring by *Glamour* and *Vanity Fair* magazines and by the organization, 100 Black Women. Hill took a year's sabbatical from her university and became a much sought-after speaker before women's groups and on college campuses.

Across the country, women began speaking out on and filing suits based on sexual harassment. Employers had to define sexual harassment and issue statements and memos about where their companies stood on the issue. The issue of sexual harassment in the workplace was permanently brought to the nation's consciousness and linked forever with the three day television "seminar" in the U.S. Senate. In the words of Julianne Malveaux, the economist, "...Sexual harassment is about power. Black men don't have that much managerial power. They can leer, but they can't lean."

In addition, the Hill-Thomas hearing galvanized women into political action to change the face of an all-white, 98 percent male senate. The elections in November 1992 brought four more women to the Senate, and twenty-four women to the House of Representatives. One new senator was Carol Mosley-Braun, a black woman from Illinois, who had enthusiastic support from women and blacks in nearly every state. The media called 1992 the Year of the Woman in politics, and much of the credit for the change went to Anita Hill.

bell hooks, in her book, *Yearning,* says "Until black men can face the reality that sexism empowers them despite the impact of racism in their lives, it will be difficult to engage in meaningful dialogue about gender. Listening to black men talk about their social reality, one often hears narratives of victimization. Even very successful black men will talk about their lives as though racism is denying them access to forms of power they cannot even describe....Historically the language used to describe the way black men are victimized within racist society has been sexualized. When words like castration, emasculation, impotency are the commonly used terms to describe the nature of black male suffering, a discursive practice is established that links black male liberation with gaining the right to participate fully within patriarchy. Embedded in this assumption is the idea that black women who are not willing to assist black men in their efforts to become patriarchs are 'the enemy.'...Until black women and men begin to seriously confront sexism in black communities, as well as within black individuals who live in predominantly white settings, we will continue to witness mounting tensions and ongoing divisiveness between the two groups. Masculinity as it is conceived within patriarchy is life-threatening to black men."

AFRICAN AMERICAN WOMEN IN DEFENSE OF OURSELVES (AAWIDOO)

ALTHOUGH IT SEEMED AT FIRST THAT HILL WAS DEFEATED IN the halls of the Senate, she gave women, and especially black women a voice, something they often had not had in this society. A month after the hearings, a group of "1,603 women of African descent" placed an ad listing all their names in major national newspapers stating, in part: "We are particularly outraged by the racist and sexist treatment of Professor Anita Hill, an African American woman who was maligned and castigated for daring to speak publicly of her own experience of sexual abuse. The malicious defamation of Professor Hill insulted all women of African descent and sent a dangerous message to any woman who might contemplate a sexual harassment complaint." The ad went on to say, "Many have erroneously portrayed the allegations against Clarence Thomas as an issue of either gender or race. As women of African descent, we understand sexual harassment as both. We further understand that Clarence Thomas outrageously manipulated the legacy of lynching in order to shelter himself from Anita Hill's allegations. To deflect attention away from the reality of sexual abuse in African American women's lives, he trivialized and misrepresented this painful part of African American people's history.

This country, which has a long legacy of racism and sexism, has never taken the abuse of Black women seriously. Throughout U.S. history Black women have been sexually stereotyped as immoral, insatiable, perverse, the initiators in all sexual contacts—abusive or otherwise. The common assumption in legal proceedings as well as in the larger society has been that Black women cannot be raped or otherwise sexually abused. As Anita Hill's experience demonstrates, Black women who speak of these matters are not likely to be believed....In 1991, we cannot tolerate this type of dismissal of any one Black woman's experience or this attack upon our collective character without protest, outrage, and resistance....We pledge ourselves to continue to speak out in defense of one another, in defense of the African American community and against those who are hostile to social justice no matter what color they are. No one will speak for us but ourselves."

Though this statement was signed by a minute portion of the nation's black women, many more would have signed had they known about it. The statement expressed the views of many. As a document of concern and intention it could serve as a manifesto for all black women who have felt exploited or wronged by any man, black or white. For the women signers and other women who agree with them, it is important that black men understand that black women will not continue to be silent in the face of the kind of harm that comes to them, to black families and the community through the Uncivil War being waged between black men and black women.

Anita Hill and Clarence Thomas were only two combatants in this war, but their case crystallized many of the issues that have black men and women at odds with each other. Thomas won that battle in that he was approved by the Senate Judiciary Committee and is now a Supreme Court Justice, in spite of Hill's charges. Only two blacks in our history have managed that achievment. Still, the charges tainted him by casting doubts on his character and his judgment. As time passes, he loses believers—Hill's credibility now outpolls his.

On the Court, Thomas has been true to his conservative line; he wrote a major anti-union ruling which barred leafletting on company property and joined in a decision that set back minority voting rights by allowing local and state governments to reallocate political power among elected officials without getting federal approval. He has also joined in opinions weakening affirmative action and minority redistricting. It is likely that he will follow the precedent he has set and will remain a black man on the country's highest court whose allegiance remains with the white conservatives who catapulted him to power.

Hill, whose conservative bent was also revealed in the infamous hearings, will have to live the rest of her life with the notoriety the case brought her. But she is also credited with awakening men and women of all colors to a problem between men and women at work that had not, to that point, been perceived as a serious, or necessarily addressable, issue by men.

The Hill-Thomas hearings also brought attention to the tightrope walked by single, well-educated, highly intelligent black women on the social and professional fronts today; the relationship, dating and marriage dilemmas they face. This condensed enactment of the Uncivil War between black men and women went to the heart of the war and exposed some of the pain and hurt such warfare brings. Nothing was resolved at the end of the hearings. But the reverberations from it will last for years to come and have given black men and black women an incentive to come to grips with their differences. A positive outcome would be if black women and men would sit around a table for peace talks. The impulse in the community is that it is time for this to occur.

CHAPTER FIVE

WAR HEROES

J
UST AS ANY WAR CAN ELICIT UNSPEAKABLE BEHAVIOR among those who are fighting or are touched by the war, it can also bring out honorable behavior in others. In the Uncivil War between black men and black women, war criminals are those whose actions and words do damage to relationships between the two. The antics of war criminals attract lots of press attention and many of them even have their defenders.

War heroes, on the other hand, are generally quieter and it's often left to others to sing their praises. Heroes in the Uncivil War have earned a place on the list because they are using their status, talents, energy and money in ways that promote healthy relationships between black women and men. These heroes are the supporters, the loyal, and the builders. The heroes who are supporters use their resources to assist members of the opposite gender in their specific challenges. The loyal heroes take advantage of every opportunity to highlight and underscore all the positive aspects of black men and black women. The builders work hard to develop institutions and images that encourage the positive self-esteem of men and/or women, enabling to deal constructively with a mate.

As often happens, there are many unsung heroes in this war—folks who work in their homes, communities or wider arenas to bring about peace and it's important that they continue doing so. Then, there are heroes whose positions bring them wider notice. Many of them are modest and probably would not call themselves heroes. They are simply doing what they believe in, doing what they must. The following is a look at a few public figures who have said and done things that have soothed the troubled waters between men and women, or at least opened the way for discussion. They care about where black women and black men are going—separately and together.

THE SUPPORTERS
Derrick A. Bell, Jr.

FORMER HARVARD LAW SCHOOL PROFESSOR, DERRICK A. BELL, Jr., has to be considered a first-class supporting hero. He decided to put his money—in fact, his annual salary—where his mouth was in April 1990. Bell, who had taught at Harvard since 1969, announced that he was taking an unpaid leave of absence (forfeiting $124,000 a year) to protest the fact that the law school did not have one tenured professor who was a woman of color. It was a bold move that stirred turmoil. Few professors had ever gone so far when they disagreed with a school's administration, but Bell had long considered himself an "inside agitator" and was known for speaking out against policies he opposed.

For a year before Bell went on leave, students at Harvard Law had appealed to the school for wider diversity among the faculty and Bell had supported their entreaties vocally. He recognized that his own hiring as the first black professor at the law school had largely been due to earlier student activism. But, he noted in a statement about his leave, "the faculty is as seriously unrepresentative now as it was before I became its first black member in 1969." Bell went on to say that his presence at Harvard Law was not enough, because "I am not able to understand, interpret, and articulate the very unique conditions and challenges black women face." So, he took his leave.

Bell's unprecedented action was the focus of national media attention and started academia talking about the issue of diversity. Harvard, however, retreated to the well-worn defense that it had tried, but simply could not find a qualified black woman to add to the law school faculty. At the time of Bell's announcement, only five women and three blacks were tenured at the law school, out of a total tenured faculty of 62.

Fighting for the rights of blacks has been a part of Bell's life since he graduated from the University of Pittsburgh Law School. He worked first in the U.S. Justice Department but quit when he was ordered to give up his membership in the National Association for the Advancement of Colored People (NAACP). From there he went to the NAACP Legal Defense and Education Fund, which was then headed by Thurgood Marshall. The legal division where Bell worked was responsible for developing most of the important law suits that would dismantle de jure segregation.

When he arrived at Harvard a few years later, Bell was personally and professionally committed to extending a helping hand to other blacks and had long lobbied to have more minority students and faculty overall at Harvard. Bell called Harvard "the oldest existing, most prestigious and, in the view of many, the best law school in the United States" in spite of its "horrible history," its exclusion of blacks and women until he arrived in 1969.

During his leave, Bell earned money from speaking engagements around the country. He also wrote the allegorical *Faces at the Bottom of the Well: The Permanence of Racism,* which was published in 1992. Bell was terminated from Harvard after his protest went on for two years. He is now a Scholar in Residence at New York University's law school and he remains firm in all his convictions and continues to work with and for black women and men who have chosen law careers.

Johnnetta B. Cole

THERE'S NO DISRESPECT INTENDED WHEN THE PRESIDENT OF Spelman College is called "Sister Prez." Appointed to the office in 1987, Dr. Johnnetta B. Cole is known for her warm, nurturing manner with her student body of some 1,750. The college's Board of Trustees evidently felt that Cole was just the person to be the first woman to lead the small, all female, historically-black, liberal arts college. In 1976 students had briefly held the Board hostage in an unsuccessful bid to get a female president named.

Under Cole's leadership, Spelman's always good reputation has expanded. In *U.S. News and World Report's* 1992 survey of the top 25 regional liberal arts colleges, Spelman ranked first in the south. It had moved up from 8th place in 1989.

Cole's doctorate is in anthropology and although she has done highly-respected fieldwork, her great love is teaching. Her job as president doesn't provide time in the classroom, but she still instructs through her writing, speeches, social activism and the causes she espouses. A measure of her influence was indicated when President-elect Bill Clinton selected Cole as chief of his transition team on education, labor, the arts and humanities and her name was often mentioned as a possible nominee for the cabinet position of Secretary of Education.

The mother of three sons, and a former professor at coed schools, the University of Massachusetts at Amherst and Hunter College in New York, Cole is as interested in supporting and encouraging males as females. Her speeches to Spelman's students refer to the need to embrace African-American men and she often tries to include their perspective on issues. As president of Spelman she is also a strong influence on the men of Spelman's brother school, Morehouse, and the coed students at Morris Brown, another historically black institution in the southern city.

Cole herself attended Fisk University, also a historically black college, before going on to study at Oberlin College in Ohio and Northwestern University in Chicago. A native of Jacksonville, Florida, where she attended segregated schools and experienced pre-civil rights Jim Crow, Cole encourages the women of Spelman to believe that there are no limits to what they can attain. For the women on campus, Cole is a living example of this. Senior Garnet Seraile of New York, says that Cole is a positive role model who's "into letting you know that you are your own person." In Cole's book of essays, *Conversations,* she challenges black women to commit themselves to political and social activism to bring change to their lives and the life of the black community.

Those who have been acquainted with Spelman pre-Cole and with-Cole note a real difference in the attitude of the students. Carolyn Odom, an alumna and chair of the corporate women's roundtable that Cole started soon after she arrived at the school, says that she senses a positive difference in the women on campus. "They have a sense of pride in themselves," Odom says. "Dr. Cole talks to them about 'sheroes' and tries to show them black women who have achieved things." Odom, who owns and runs a marketing and public relations firm, Creative Communication Options, in New York City also points to the 37 percent of the school body who are now involved in community outreach programs that work with drug addicted babies, prison inmates, abused women, and tutorials for public school students. "Spelman women used to have an image of being elitist, but we've always had concerned women on campus," says Odom, recalling her own participation in civil rights demonstrations when she was a student in the 1970s.

Shortly after assuming the presidency, Cole married for a second time. Her first husband was white economist Robert Cole, whom she met in graduate school. They were married for 22 years and had three sons. Cole's present husband, Arthur J. Robinson, Jr., a black man, is a familiar presence on the Spelman campus. In fact, he started coaching a school tennis team, a first. Robinson, a retired public health service administrator with two sons from an earlier marriage, was actually a childhood sweetheart of Cole's.

According to an essay that Robinson wrote for the July 1990 issue of *Essence* magazine, their marriage works because the two of them take the time to have "honest and painful talks" that have established trust between them and affirmed a commitment to nurturing their special relationship. Alumna Odom believes that the "loving, supportive" Cole-Robinson partnership sets a good example for the young women on the campus.

Cole's marriage is also an example of how it is possible for blacks to marry successfully the second time, even if their first marriage has ended in divorce. Like many of the partners mentioned in this chapter, Cole and her husband, instead of listening to the statistics about black marriages and their divorce rates, decided to give another relationship a chance.

THE LOYAL
Denzel Washington

JUST PRIOR TO THE TELECAST OF THE 1993 ACADEMY AWARDS show, Barbara Walters interviewed Denzel Washington, a nominee for Best Actor for his brilliant portrayal of Malcolm X. Washington did not win another Oscar that night, but he did move up another notch in the eyes of millions of already-adoring black women, and many others, for the tributes he gave his wife and mother in response to Walters' questions.

Washington told Walters that Pauletta, his wife and mother of his four children, was the backbone of their family. He vowed before a worldwide audience to never leave her. "She might leave me," he said, but he was committed to staying in the relationship.

It's rare that American audiences get to hear a black male celebrity, especially one who is at the top of his profession as Washington is, praise his black wife. It is almost a cliche that black men who achieve stardom no longer find black women satisfactory as mates. Many of these stars will leave their black wives and marry, or exclusively date, white women. (For more on this phenomenon, see chapter 5, "War Criminals.")

The apparent rejection of black women by significant numbers of high-profile achievers is a difficult image for black women to combat and makes them appear undesirable in the marriage market even to the non-celebrity black men who also want to marry "up" and who now have more opportunities to meet, date and wed white women than in the past.

These changing circumstances give the remarks of Denzel Washington special weight and make him a high-profile loyal hero in the Uncivil Wars. Washington met Pauletta Pearson, a talented concert pianist and singer, early in his career and they are raising a family in Los Angeles. It's not that he necessarily set out to be a role model as a black actor or family man. It's just happening that way.

Actually, Washington gives a lot of the credit to his mother—and his Pentecostal preacher father—for the man he's become. His parents divorced when he was fourteen and Washington remained with his mother in Mt. Vernon, New York. When Washington began venting his frustration and anger in school and in the streets, he said in an interview, "My mom's love for me and her desire for me to do well kept me out of trouble." His father was also a strong influence, imparting a sense of responsibility, integrity and a respect for hard work. By the late 1980s, Washington was getting the kind of recognition and box-office approval given to only a handful of black men ever. His good looks and sex appeal earned him the attention of female fans of all ages and races. Married in 1982, Washington has maintained a balance between his image as a Hollywood sex symbol and a faithful and loving husband.

Although Washington was not responsible for the writing in *The Mighty Quinn,* the first movie in which he had a starring role, black audiences held their collective breath when a white femme fatale propositioned him. When he turned her down some blacks in the audience cheered and others applauded. Denzel had stayed true to his screen wife, and symbolically, to all black women.

The accolades that Washington gave his wife on Oscar night were not isolated. Again and again in interviews he has said approximately the same thing. He told an interviewer for the *New York Times,* in 1992, "My wife probably has as much to do with my success and my talent as anybody, because I may have gone astray had it not been for her." He added, "Maybe I would have started getting caught up in the limousines, parties and all the other stuff. But she's the rock in our marriage."

Danny Glover

DANNY GLOVER IS ANOTHER POPULAR ACTOR WHO TAKES advantage of the opportunities provided to him to highlight the positive aspects of African Americans. In 1985, Danny Glover played one of the cruelest black men ever to be seen on a movie screen, the role of "Mister" in Steven Spielberg's film version of Alice Walker's novel, *The Color Purple.* Controversy and much discussion was created everywhere the film was shown. Walker had already been accused of creating a monster, an unyielding, unredeemable black man who exploited and mistreated the young woman he had made his wife. Mister's frustration, fear and anger also poisoned his relations with his father, his son and his sister-in-law, whom he tried to rape.

Although most viewers were able to separate the actor from the role he played, Glover came under some fire for his convincing portrayal. Perhaps because he had to understand the character's motivation, Glover looked deep into Mister's mind and soul. In talking about the complexity of Mister, Glover said, "His insensitivity comes out of a rigid, limited overview of himself and the world he had to deal with....A lot of what Mister does comes out of his own pain." The character abused his wife, Glover thought, because he felt abused by the world. Glover's analysis did not excuse the behavior, but only attempted to explain it.

If anything, Danny Glover is the polar opposite of Mister. Married since 1976 to his wife Asake, a singer and owner of a San Francisco art gallery, Glover is a loving husband and devoted father to their teenage daughter Mandisa. A native of San Francisco and a former student activist at San Francisco State University, Glover worked in the Black Panthers' Breakfast for Children program in the 1960s and helped organize a strike against the university when it tried to end its ethnic studies program. He was also involved in tutorial programs at the city's elementary schools and worked with community people who had been displaced by urban development.

Although his acting career takes up much of his energy now, Glover still devotes time to young blacks in the city and around the country. He tours every month to talk to youth about the importance of education, the dangers of drugs, and other topics of interest to them. Glover's commitment to black people goes beyond the U.S. to Africa. He is one of several investors in New Age Beverages, a South African business venture that will initially provide 200 jobs to produce and distribute Pepsi-Cola products.

Glover's body of work, which includes roles as Nelson Mandela, the new president of South Africa, in an HBO movie, and as a police officer in the action-packed series of *Lethal Weapon* movies, has earned him superstar status. Glover is also branching out into production and directing. His own company, Carrie Productions, co-produced and he starred in the critically acclaimed, *To Sleep With Anger,* a Charles Burnett film.

Glover has made it in a field where few blacks attain his standing. His head and heart, however, have kept him grounded and committed to giving back to his family and community.

THE BUILDERS
Haki R. Madhubuti

HAKI MADHUBUTI IS A BUILDER, PUBLISHER, POET, ESSAYIST, professor, thinker, race man. Madhubuti is all that, and more. Known as Don L. Lee in the 1960s, Madhubuti's was a poetic voice that clearly and loudly spoke of his vision for black people. His poetry resounded with love for, and was an exhortation to, the community.

Madhubuti's poetry and, later, his record as the publisher of Third World Press in Chicago and a founder of an elementary school in that city, has been a call to nationalism. He describes and ascribes to "real nationalism—that which embodies culture, politics, defense, and economics...a nationalism that will draw brothers and sisters into self and not alienate them; will answer questions and not only present problems; will build people not individuals, with leadership qualities...a community of leaders—not just followers—who can and will work together."

Madhubuti's serious concern for future generations of blacks is evident in the books he has published since starting his company in 1967 (it is the oldest continually operating African American book publisher in the U. S.). He is the author of one of Third World Press's best sellers, *Black Men: Obsolete, Single, Dangerous? Afrikan-American* [sic] Families in Transition. In that book he devotes a couple of chapters to black male-female relationships and the importance of these relationships to black families and the community (the chapters are titled, "Before Sorry: Listening to and Feeling the Flow of Black Women," and "What's a Daddy? Marriage and Fathering").

Madhubuti's company has also published thoughtful works by other authors on issues close to the hearts and minds of black people, including *The Isis Papers: The Keys to the Colors* by Howard University Professor Frances Cress-Welsing, and *The Destruction of Black Civilization* by Chancellor Williams.

Prolific and profound, Madhubuti gives his whole self to pursuits that will move black people forward. A father of five and an inspiration to the thousands with whom he's come in contact or who have read his works, Madhubuti was himself nurtured and encouraged as a young poet and friend by Chicago resident and Illinois Poet Laureate Gwendolyn Brooks. Today, Brooks is published by Third World Press.

Safisha Madhubuti, mother of Haki's three youngest children, is a writer, educator and founder, with her husband and others, of the New Concept Development Center for elementary education. The Madhubutis view their work for the community as part of the bond that has strengthened their own union. In a 1991 interview with *Essence* magazine Madhubuti talked about the value of their joint work and of his commitment to his family—"there's nothing more important to me than them," he said.

Madhubuti's vision only begins with his family. It extends outward to embrace the larger community in Chicago and across the country. He has written that "As a people is the only way we can endure and black-nation building must accelerate at top speed." As he writes, so he lives.

Bill and Camille Cosby

CAMILLE COSBY SUPPORTED HER HUSBAND BILL WHEN HE moved the family (they have four daughters and a son) from California to Massachusetts in the early 1970s so that he could pursue a doctorate in education. She is as committed as he is to higher education and went on to earn her own doctorate degree in 1992. Camille serves as Vice President for the Cosby Company, the family business, and is active in all its enterprises. The Cosby's have been married for 30 years and have managed to keep their lives relatively private despite their enormous fortune and Bill's fame.

Bill Cosby probably used some situations from his own family in his television show, as he does in his stand-up comedy routines, but he has always made it known that his wife and his family come first in his life and that he is devoted to them. He is also devoted to education and has put his money where his mouth is. Nothing speaks louder of this commitment than his and Camille's $20 million gift to Spelman College in 1988; plus they had already been regular donors to a number of black colleges. At the time, their donation was the largest single gift ever to a black college. The reason for the gift, Cosby told reporters, was that "Mrs. Cosby and I have been blessed because I found a vein of gold in the side of a mountain." The only other comment he made was that he and his wife wanted Johnnetta Cole to know how much they loved the school. One of the Cosby daughters, and thousands of black women have received an outstanding education there. The Cosbys also donated $1.8 million to the National Council of Negro Women in 1994 toward the establishment of a National Center for African-American Women.

The vein of gold that Cosby struck were two hit television sitcoms that he created, "The Cosby Show" and the spinoff, "A Different World," which was set at a fictional black college. "The Cosby Show" premiered in the fall of 1984 and for its first four seasons was the top-rated show on television, single-handedly reviving the floundering sitcom format. The show ran for eight years, reached millions of homes in the U.S. and overseas, and made Cosby one of the highest-paid entertainers in the world—he led *Forbes* magazine's 1992 list of 40 "filthy rich and famous" celebrities, with total gross earnings for 1991 and 1992 of $98 million.

Cosby's television middle-class black family featured an obstetrician dad, Cliff Huxtable (played by Cosby), his lawyer wife Claire, and five children. The resemblance to Cosby's own family of five offspring was more than coincidental and events from his real life sometimes inspired what happened in his reel life. The Huxtable family lived comfortably in a Brooklyn brownstone.

There were grumblings from some critics in both the black and the white communities that the show did not accurately portray black life in America. But supporters of the show pointed out that there is a solid black middle class in this country many of whom earn enough to afford the kind of lifestyle the Huxtables enjoyed. "The Cosby Show" was an alternate, and for many a welcome, view of black family life, where parents and children could exhibit love, respect and friendship for each other without at the same time having to cope with grinding poverty and violent crime.

Both "The Cosby Show" and "A Different World" provided weekly showcases of authentic black art, literature and history. Props for the two shows included paintings and prints that boosted the careers of black artists, black magazines and books and references to and portraits of major figures in African American history. At one point Cosby threatened to leave the show when NBC asked that the "Free South Africa" sign be removed from the door of Theo Huxtable's room because it was "too controversial." Cosby stayed and so did the sign.

There may have been differences of opinion and different approaches to solving problems within the Huxtable household, but there was none of the usual insulting or belittling exchanges between family members that has been the standard form of communication on black sitcoms. There were lots of laughs, but not at the expense of the parents or the children.

Earnings from his television work have permitted the Cosbys to give financial support to causes they believe are worthy. Their contributions to black colleges have set an example that other African American entertainers and businesspeople are following. And thousands of young black men and women are the beneficiaries of their generosity.

Ossie Davis and Ruby Dee

RUBY DEE AND OSSIE DAVIS HAVE BEEN MARRIED FOR 45 YEARS. That is quite an achievement for anyone, let alone a couple in the entertainment business. But they are not just entertainers, they believe in black people as well as in themselves. Throughout their long and formidable careers, they have managed to carefully sift their roles so that they did not appear in any productions that stereotyped or degraded African Americans. On the contrary, they have worked long and hard to promote those efforts that contribute to the positive self–image of black people. Dee got Alex Haley together with David Wolper to make the ground–breaking television series, *Roots.* Together, Dee and Davis coproduced and acted in *Countdown at Kusini,* the Delta Sigma Theta feature film shot entirely in Africa by African Americans. Davis and Dee have been an integral part of the black liberation struggle actively working with controversial figures long before it became fashionable. Martin Luther King Jr., Paul Robeson and W.E.B. Dubois were among the leaders with whom they shared a vision. Davis's eulogy of Malcolm X has become a classic in the black community. According to the December, 1994 *Essence,* Dee and

Davis have said they belong as much to the struggle as to each other. In the same piece, Davis and Dee generously share the determined effort that kept their marriage going. Davis was quoted as saying "I wasn't about to let my manhood or my maleness put me in a position where I would have to say good–bye to Ruby...If Ruby wanted to leave home, I would say, `Ruby leave, but take me with you.' Somehow I was going to work that thing out." And Dee offered, "Well, I made up my mind that, given infidelity, I would have to do battle. Because I'm not willing to let this man go for any such reason. I want him. So if you want something, you put your weight on it. You just get in there and fight for it." And that sums up the apparent philosophy of Dee and Davis for their lives and their marriage: "Just get in there and fight."

Fortunately, there are many other well-known African Americans who use their talents, energy and money to promote healthy relationships between black men and women and to support the black community. Not all of them can be included here, but mention should be made of Barbara and Earl Graves, Sr., of *Black Enterprise* magazine and Julius and Turquoise Erving who developed a Pepsi bottling business providing jobs in Washington, D.C.; Susan L. Taylor and Kephra Burns and Nathan and Julia Hare, two husband/wife writing teams whose material contributes to increased knowledge about African-Americans; and Michael and Juanita Jordan of the Jordan Foundation that contributed millions to build a much-needed Boys and Girls Club in one of Chicago's poorest black neighborhoods.

These are all people worth emulating.

CHAPTER SIX

WAR CRIMINALS

WAR HAS A WAY OF STRIPPING THINGS DOWN TO bare essentials. Conflict makes clear who is noble and who is not, which women are selfish, which men are givers, who will die for a brother or sister and who will endanger their lives. War produces heroes and it also breeds criminals—men and women who commit despicable acts for their own, or someone else's gain. War separates out those who will betray family, friends, tribe or country for a price, or out of apathy or ignorance.

The war between black men and women is no different. As in other conflicts, the criminals in this Uncivil War capture and dominate the spotlight. Perhaps it's because their bold, outrageous language or behavior fascinate us, even while we're horrified. War criminals seem somehow larger than life—moral outlaws without feelings of guilt or shame.

The criminals are of several types: the abusers, the self-absorbed, and the traitors. Abuse of the opposite sex can be verbal, as in some of the worst rap music; or physical, as demonstrated by those who batter their mates and/or threaten them with bodily harm. The self-absorbed are perhaps the most numerous of the "criminal" types. These are the folks whose only perception of any situation is how it affects their own personal desires. No one else's feelings, views or well-being is taken into consideration. Traitors feel no allegiance to the people with whom they share a heritage and are willing to vilify and/or stereotype their own people if they believe they can benefit in some way from doing so.

Those who have been labelled war criminals in this chapter are included here because of their negative behavior towards black women or black men or both. Black male celebrities — politicians, entertainers, sports figures—dominate this chapter because readers will recognize their names and be familiar with their exploits. Also high-profile males have a combination of power, million dollar incomes and fame that few black women, except perhaps Oprah Winfrey, ever achieve.

A certain arrogance is sometimes acquired along with the money and power making some people feel that the rules and limitations that govern most people are nullified for them, particularly when it comes to personal relationships. The white male-dominated press also seems to relish the indiscretions of rich and/or famous black males, so their sexual escapades, drug problems and encounters with the police are closely scrutinized and written about, usually in sensational headlines. This same intense observation is not visited on whites of any gender or on rich and/or famous black women. Still, there are a few celebrity women who have earned inclusion on our list of war criminals.

It's not just celebrities or public figures who deserve to be considered war criminals. There are many "unknown" perpetrators of war crimes. The term can be applied to those women who don't differentiate one man from another, but bitterly declare "black men ain't shit," or "all men are dogs." The hard line that they take leaves no room for compromise or negotiation with men in the Uncivil War.

War criminal should also be used to describe men who casually and regularly refer to women as "hoes" (whores) or bitches. Calling women by these names is not a new thing; there have always been some black men who have done it. It is hurt, anger and low self-esteem that lets a man use this kind of derogatory language for a black woman. Because he places little value on himself, he devalues his woman and sees her as someone to be scorned and called "out of her name."

In the last decade, ugly put-downs and name calling, most aimed at black women, have come out of the closet to be aired in print, on recordings and videos, on talk radio and cable television. This kind of outspoken, kiss-my-ass attitude demeans all blacks and prolongs the Uncivil War between men and women. Those who are most guilty, those who set the worst examples should be named and denounced for the damage they've done. This chapter doesn't provide an exhaustive list, it just provides the names and stories of some of the most identifiable offenders, male and female.

THE ABUSERS
Mike Tyson

IT MAY SEEM REDUNDANT TO CALL EX-HEAVYWEIGHT BOXING champion Mike Tyson a war criminal since he actually served three years of a six-year term for rape in an Indiana prison. What earns Tyson inclusion in this chapter is his history of physically abusive behavior toward women from his adolescence up to the time of the rape charge.

In the film documentary "Fallen Champ: The Untold Story of Mike Tyson", Teddy Atlas, a trainer at the D'Amato camp who worked with Tyson when he was still an amateur, states that Tyson got into trouble at Catskill High School in New York. "He'd verbally, and a little physically, force himself on girls...there were a whole bunch of incidents reported...by young girls in school. They'd say no. He'd get emotional. He felt he had a right to act that way."

Later, as a young, single and very rich black male, Tyson found himself being propositioned and pursued by scores of women. Tyson was coarse and boorish with women apparently not understanding that there were limits even for him. Accusations and lawsuits stemming from his behavior began to pile up in the mid-1980s. In February 1986 he made sexual propositions to a saleswoman in an Albany shopping mall and became abusive when she turned him down. No charges were filed against him by the woman or the store. Later on the same day he propositioned a woman in a movie theater and was thrown out. Again, no charges were filed. In June 1987 Tyson tried to kiss an unwilling female parking lot employee and hit a male attendant at the same lot. For this altercation he was charged with misdemeanor assault and battery and assault with a deadly weapon. Tyson settled out of court for a reported $105,000.

In February of 1988 Tyson married actress Robin Givens. Four months into the marriage, Givens publicly stated that Tyson had beaten her. Possibly more damaging than Givens' charge of domestic violence was former world light-heavy-weight champion and sportswriter Jose Torres' biography, *Fire & Fear: The Inside Story of Mike Tyson.* In the book Tyson was quoted as saying that the best punch he had ever thrown was when Robin "offended me and I went 'bam,' and she flew backward, hitting every fucking wall in the apart-ment." Torres' book also quoted Tyson as saying, "I like to hurt women when I make love to them. I like to hear them scream with pain, to see them bleed. It gives me pleasure." Tyson has called Torres' account absurd and denied that he enjoys hurting women.

For a man with Tyson's history of abusive encounters with the opposite sex, probably the last place he should have been invited to was a beauty pageant where he could interact with fifty beautiful young women. Tyson was invited to the Miss Black America Pageant in Indianapolis by organizers of the event. Desiree Washington's rape charge was the most damag-ing made against him as a result of his presence at the pageant, but it was not the only accusation.

Rosie Jones, Miss Black America 1990, who was present at the 1991 pageant, filed a $100 million lawsuit against Tyson for allegedly assaulting, battering and humiliating her by grab-bing her buttocks during the opening ceremony. The suit was settled out of court for an undisclosed amount. The director of the pageant, J. Morris Anderson, filed a $21 million lawsuit which called Tyson a "serial buttocks fondler" who fondled or sexually insulted at least 10 of the beauty contestants. Anderson's suit was later dropped.

Tyson's loyal supporters have pointed out that his wealth and fame made him an easy target for women who had no qualms about using their bodies to get next to him. Although this is true, what Tyson needs is counseling to help him learn appropriate behavior so that he can cope with the women he will again encounter now that he is out of prison. Most of all, he has to understand that his fame and money don't give him the right to abuse even the women that clamor for his attention.

Darryl Strawberry

NEW YORK YANKEES OUTFIELDER DARRYL STRAWBERRY, 32, is considered one of the most phenomenal ball players of this era. Originally signed to play with the New York Mets in 1984, his outstanding play earned Rookie of the Year honors.

But Strawberry has also made headlines since January 1990 for his problems with his wives and other women. Early in 1990, his first wife Lisa (who had accused him of breaking her nose in 1986) called police to their home in Encino, California. She alleged that Strawberry struck her during a heated argument, knocked her to the floor and pulled a handgun on her. The police held him in jail for a couple of hours. Lisa did not press charges against her husband. However, they later divorced.

In September 1993, Strawberry's live-in-lover, Charisse Simon called police to their residence, claiming he had punched her. He was taken to jail for 90 minutes and released on bail. Five days after the event, Simon opted not to press charges and they were married three months later.

Strawberry seems prone to physically abusing the women in his life. The light punishment he received and the fact that the women did not press charges, which is the pattern in most cases of abused women, did not give Strawberry any incentive to seek help for this problem. In the spring of 1994 Strawberry publicly admitted that he had an alcohol and drug abuse problem and would seek treatment at a rehabilitation center.

Robin Givens

MIKE TYSON WAS RIPE FOR THE PICKING BY THE BRIGHT, ambitious starlet, Robin Givens. A graduate of preppie Sarah Lawrence College in New York, Givens' early celebrity profiles say that she was discovered by Bill Cosby, who persuaded her to leave Harvard Medical School for a career in show business. The truth is, Givens was never enrolled at the Ivy League medical school, but she certainly was more educated than the boxer she chose for her first marriage.

Whatever her motives were for marrying Tyson, it wasn't long before she publicly voiced her regrets and did so in ways that were particularly demeaning. During their turbulent eight-month marriage, Tyson appeared to come apart at the seams, wrecking luxury cars (a Bentley and a BMW) and getting into explosive brawls with Givens and others—in particular, her mother Ruth Roper.

In the brief span of the Tyson-Givens marriage, Robin and Roper confronted Tyson's white manager, Bill Cayton, over his contracts with the fighter and their financial arrangements. Some observers saw the women as looking out for Tyson's best interests, but others saw it as clear evidence that Robin herself wanted to get control of her husband's money. The dispute eventually drew in boxing promoter Don King, and a host of lawyers. The case was settled with Cayton retaining control of Tyson's career until 1992 but having his manager's share lowered from 33 1/3 to 20 percent.

While Tyson was caught up in this dispute, he and Givens were still having marital problems. Givens exacerbated the situation, playing into the hands of the media and exposing Tyson's weaknesses for all to see. In one New York Post story Givens talked about her husband's mental problems: "He's been manic-depressive for many years and they [his old boxing family] have been ignoring it. Michael takes a great deal of protecting..." Givens said that she and Roper saw that Tyson kept appointments with Harlem Hospital-based black psychiatrist Dr. Henry L. McCurtis.

Givens shrewdly used television and the tabloids to help build a case against Tyson. In a September 1988 interview on ABC television's "20/20," Tyson sat beside Givens mute and looking sedated while she told Walters and a worldwide audience of millions that living with Tyson for the previous seven months had been "pure hell, worse than anything I could imagine." She also said that Tyson could not control his temper and repeated her assertion that he was a manic depressive. When outraged Tyson fans and others reacted to Givens' appearance on the show, she did a follow-up where she said her comments about Tyson weren't meant as an insult. "If I offended anyone, I apologize."

A week after the show, Givens filed for divorce. In her divorce petition Givens painted herself as the hapless victim of a "violent and physically abusive" man who was "prone to unprovoked rages of violence and destruction." A month later she sued Tyson for $125 million, charging libel because she said Tyson called her and her mother, among other things, "the slime of the slime."

Givens left her marriage several millions of dollars richer than when she entered it. That's not a crime; gold-digging may be the world's second oldest profession. But Givens deserves to be called a war criminal for the way she manipulated her husband in the media.

THE SELF-ABSORBED
Marion Barry

MANY CRIMINALS IN THE UNCIVIL WAR BETWEEN BLACK MEN and women blame their negative behavior on an addiction to alcohol, drugs or sex. Washington, D.C., mayor Marion Barry claims his life, for a while, was dominated by all three. Before these addictions brought him to disgrace and a six-month jail term, Barry had distinguished himself as political activist-turned-political power broker.

Barry was the first national chairman of the Student National Coordinating Committee (SNCC) and was a major figure in the organization's voting rights push in the South in the 1960s. He served as mayor of the nation's capital for twelve years, 1978 to 1990. Almost from the start of his administration, however, rumors began circulating of extra-marital sexual escapades, drug use and mismanagement of public funds. Barry dismissed these allegations and his reputation as a black leader remained intact.

Barry's downfall came when a long-time mistress and one-time drug supplier, model Hazel "Rasheeda" Moore, took part in an FBI sting operation that led to his arrest for cocaine possession in January 1990.

As the sordid tale of Barry's years of substance abuse unfolded during his court trial, a portrait emerged of the mayor as an emotional batterer of women. Both his wife, Effi, and his mistress were manipulated by Barry to meet his insatiable need for drugs and sex. Under threat of a possible perjury charge, Hazel Moore finally betrayed Barry. "The bitch set me up!" he was heard to exclaim as he was taken into custody, and residents and tourists alike later sported T shirts with that quote. Barry's wife stood with him through the humiliating trial, but she left him soon after and moved out of the city. Their 14-year marriage ended in divorce early in 1993. Barry has remarried and been reelected as mayor of D.C. But it is his earlier self-indulgent behavior toward the women in his life that earns him a place in this chapter on war criminals.

THE TRAITORS

ALTHOUGH 95% OF BLACKS MARRY OTHER BLACKS, THERE ARE many in the black community who feel that there should be no male-female relationships between whites and blacks not only because of our history, but because racism and prejudice are still very much evident in our society. These people are offended whenever they see interracial couples, especially when the black member of those couples is rich and famous. When Jack

Johnson, the first black to win the world heavyweight boxing championship in 1908, wooed and won white women, it was considered an act of defiance. Today, among many, it is considered an act of betrayal.

There are several reasons why black men turn to white women once they achieve a certain status, but the major one may be that successful men want "trophy wives," women who are highly prized and admired for their beauty and feminine attributes. If she's intelligent, wealthy or famous herself, that only adds to her status—and his. By American standards, promoted through television, films and the advertising industry, the woman who best fits this standard is a white woman, preferably blond, although an occasional brunette is considered okay. When a black man wins one of these "trophies," he is showing white men and black men that he is a winner in the competition among men for women. Against all odds he has obtained what this society considers its best.

Whether intentionally or not, these preferences for white women send a clear message to black women that they are not worthy, that they do not measure up as a prize for the successful black man. It is a repeat of a message black women have heard all their lives: they are not pretty enough, smart enough, witty enough, slim enough, or white enough. Black women realize that there is no way they can match the fantasy so many black men hold, so their self-esteem suffers.

Black celebrities who never seem to find lovers among their own race and repeatedly marry or have liaisons only with whites are subject to particular derision. A classic example of this is O.J. Simpson, who after divorcing his black wife, seemed never to look at another black woman. Diana Ross has been married twice, both times to white men. Whoopi Goldberg is never seen with black men or musician Quincy Jones with black women. Michael Jackson's few public "dates" were with white women, and when he married, he chose the white daughter of Elvis Presley, a highly-prized "trophy."

Among those celebrities who currently have non-black sig-

nificant others are actors/ entertainers Harry Belafonte, Dia-
hann Carroll, Rosie Grier, Gregory Hines, Al Jarreau, James
Earl Jones, Sidney Poitier, Lionel Richie, Billy Dee Williams,
Montel Williams, Alfre Woodard; athletes Bill Russell and
Frank Thomas; fashion model, Iman; Julian Bond, former
Georgia state senator; and singer, Tina Turner.

Mark Mathabane, the black South African writer who lives
in the U.S. and is married to a white woman says, "Interracial
couples have an important role to play in the improvement of
race relations. They know firsthand the importance of blacks
and whites knowing each other as individuals rather than
through stereotypes and half-truths."

More importantly, however, may be that the ability to have a
happy relationship is so hard to come by that, no matter the
race of the partner, achieving that rare state is what is most to
be desired.

Wilt Chamberlain

BASKETBALL GREAT WILT CHAMBERLAIN TOOK THIS ATTITUDE
towards black women a step further than most by publicly stating his contempt in his autobiography. Chamberlain stands
head and shoulders above most men, on and off the playing
court and no one can take a thing away from his athletic feats.
His name, however is infamous among many for his statements
in the 1973 book, *Wilt,* and his boasts about his sexual prowess
in his 1991 memoir, *The View from Above.* Like other black
men who have made it to the top of their professions, Chamberlain intimates that white women suit his lifestyle more than
black women. In *Wilt,* he wrote:

"I would imagine that compatibility is another reason I date
more white girls than black girls...for a black man I've been
very fortunate. I have a good education and I've traveled
extensively, and I've become a knowledgeable businessman;
I've learned to appreciate good food and good art—the good
life....Most blacks—women even more than men—haven't
been that lucky. They don't have my experience and sophisti-

cation. So understandably, many of them are not good companions—or lovers—for me....Because so many black families have been forced to live in crowded hovels, with mother and father and four little kids all sleeping in the same small room, sex has often been something done as quickly and quietly as possible—and preferably, in the dark. As a result, many black girls grow up thinking of sex as furtive and dirty, and they can't respond as fully as they should to a man."

With his education, sophistication and extensive travel, it's surprising that Chamberlain hasn't encountered some of the thousands of black women who can match his educational background and cultural experience and who did not grow up in a hovel. When Chamberlain attended Kansas State University from 1956 to 1958; black female college students outnumbered black males by about 50,000. There were 136,000 black male graduates in 1960, the year he would have graduated, and 176,000 black female graduates. Many of these women have gone on to distinguish themselves in the fields of business, civic affairs and the arts.

Chamberlain should have used his education for some objective, rather than subjective, research on black women's sexuality. His comments on black women appear to be nothing more than a weak rationalization for his preference for white women, which is his business, but it certainly isn't necessary for him to belittle black women in the process.

Whoopi Goldberg

WHOOPI GOLDBERG HAS BEEN A PARADOX SINCE SHE FIRST gained prominence with a one-woman show on Broadway in the early 1980s. Here was a sister who wore dreadlocks, but had adopted a Jewish surname (Whoopi's birth name is Karen Johnson). Blacks wondered, "is she one of us, or what?"

A one-time New York City welfare mom, Goldberg had earned her comedian stripes in stand-up comedy clubs. One of her funniest bits was a take-off of a blond, Southern California "Valley Girl." Hers was not so much the typical black humor, but blacks were happy to see a sister make a name for herself in the entertainment industry. Goldberg's first movie role as Celie in Stephen Spielberg's *The Color Purple,* won her plaudits for her acting. After a few commercial screen flops, Goldberg struck it rich with *Sister Act,* one of 1992's top-grossing movies.

There was uneasiness among some in the black community, though, with her penchant for white men—she married and divorced two, and in 1993 took television star Ted Danson as her lover. However, most black folks felt that to be her own business until October 8, 1993, when Danson appeared on the dais with Goldberg at her Friars Club roast in New York City in minstrel-style blackface.

(Blackface is a throwback to a time when black men were maliciously caricatured by white actors in minstrel shows. Most people consider it a racist and demeaning practice, and it was eliminated from American stages six decades ago.)

A Friars Club roast is usually open only to entertainers who are members of the club and their invited guests. The press is banned from the roasts at which friends and colleagues bombard the guest-of-honor with bawdy, off-color jokes and insults about his or her race, religion, marriage, sex life or career.

Goldberg's roast followed tradition, but on the morning after, a photograph of Danson in top hat and blackface appeared on front pages across the country. In the photo, Goldberg was seated beside him, looking up at him adoringly with a huge smile. It was obvious that she appreciated his act and she later told reporters that she had, in fact, helped to write Danson's stream of racial and sexual insults.

Blacks were outraged at the image of Whoopi looking approvingly at the blackened face of Danson, and appalled at the story about his presentation. One New York accountant said, "I felt denigrated as a woman and as a black. No man, black or white, especially white, could say those things to me in private, and certainly not before an audience."

Additional response from the black community was loud,

indignant and immediate, but Goldberg seemed surprised at the uproar. She was unapologetic, pointing out that the comments were never meant to be heard by the general public. She also explained that she had no problem with the Friars Club tradition, as a black or as a woman. Goldberg was quoted in the New York Daily News of October 9, as saying after the roast, "Nigger, nigger, nigger. Whitey, whitey, whitey. It takes a whole lot of [courage] to come out in blackface, in front of 3,000 [people]. I don't care if you don't like it. I do."

In spite of her bravado, Goldberg had to speak again, and again, about the roast. She and Danson were blasted in columns and editorials in the black and white press for being insensitive and somewhat naive for not understanding how offensive his presentation had been. Then, the *New York Observer* published what it said were excerpts of Danson's remarks, co-written by Goldberg, that had been "ferreted out" by an unidentified reporter who had been at the roast, despite the press ban. The Transom column by Frank DiGiacomo included these snippets: "Our first fight was over a Disney film called 'The Nigger Lover.' Miss Diva insisted on being the nigger. But I told her, you always play the nigger." And, "I took her up to the bedroom and fucked the shit out of her. She gave me some of that monkey love she's so famous for." Danson also offered this description of the comedian's vagina, "[It's] wider than South Africa, and twice as inflamed."

This alleged transcript and other press leaks added fuel to what had become a four-alarm fire. Goldberg and Danson were roasted again, this time in the court of public opinion. There was even talk of boycotting their movies, and customers at one Harlem video store trashed copies of *Made in America*, in which Danson and Goldberg co-starred. Finally, the two were compelled to appear together on the Black Entertainment Television network to explain Danson's act and Goldberg's part in it. Both wanted to stop the flood of criticism which had started to consume their lives.

Responsibility for the entire fiasco has to be Goldberg's. As a black woman who fought hard to overcome stereotypes about her looks and value, and as one of the few black female super-stars, she should have been more conscious of how explosive Danson's blackface act would be, even though it was performed before an audience closed to the public. (New York Mayor David Dinkins, comedian Bob Goldthwaite, and talk show host Montel Williams, who also appeared on the dais, all expressed shock and anger at Danson and Goldberg, although other pre-senters said they were not offended.)

Goldberg said it took courage for Danson to come out in blackface; but courage would have been saying, "no thanks" to a Friars roast, knowing how it could be. And if she wanted so badly to be "roasted," courage would have been finding a skit that did not pander to reminiscences of the brutal exploitation suffered by blacks at the hands of whites.

Goldberg's defense was, "I don't find black face offensive. It's a part of a history that I am a product of." And Associated Press quoted her as saying, "This is Whoopi. I never promised to be politically correct for anybody."

In October, 1994, Goldberg married her third white husband, a union labor organizer.

Shahrazad Ali

TO HER CREDIT, THE POPULARITY OF SHAHRAZAD ALI'S BOOK, *The Blackman's Guide to Understanding the Blackwoman,* did focus a spotlight on the stress between black men and women. But her credit for the book, self-published in 1990, has to be tempered once it is discovered that it is mostly a diatribe against black women, blaming them for all the problems black men face.

Ali's theories are based largely on her interviews with men in prison (one came forward to say he was her legal husband although she says she's the widow of a previous mate). Her views are misogynistic and sound remarkably like those of the most dedicated Ku Klux Klanners. According to Ali, black women are, for the most part, dirty and sex-crazed, have smaller brains than black men, and too often spew words so obscene that men have no other choice than to smack them across the mouth. Black women, Ali says, have usurped their men's positions as heads-of-household and need to step down and once again treat men with the respect that is rightfully theirs.

Black men come off no better than black women. Ali writes about them in the same simplistic, stereotypical way she writes about women. Neither gender is allowed all their complexity. Just as she degrades the black woman, Ali believes the black man should be responsible for his own behavior as well as that of the black woman. What Ali writes is sheer nonsense and some excerpts make that obvious.

On how black men should deal with black women: "The Blackman will never be able to excel until he gets his woman under control. Currently he spars with the white man to preserve his freedom while scuffling with the Blackwoman to defend his wounded manhood....His work to bring the Blackwoman into submission must begin accordingly. It is likened to stepping into the ring with a wild savage boar, a reckless fire-breathing dragon that must be tamed if the Black family is to survive. It is the Blackman's responsibility to win this battle."

On the "high class" black woman: "She is the modern girlfriend, believes she is completely self-sufficient, and is not particularly interested in keeping house, cooking dinner every night or treating the Blackman with special accord....Because she is so concerned about public opinion and what 'they' think she will customarily deal with a Blackman whom she is not particularly interested in just to have an escort on her arm. She is a rat who behaves like a dog while purring like a cat."

You get the picture. One thing no one seemed to consider is that perhaps Ali was writing about her own experiences and events in the lives of the women she knows. Unfortunately, many people took her words to be generally accurate for all black women. A lot of black men, especially young, angry ones, adopted Ali's book as scripture. In the months after its publication it set off a firestorm of discussion and argument among blacks of all generations.

The book did get blacks talking, but most of it was divisive and allowed men to place all the blame for problems in their relationships and marriages on women. Ali deserves a place of honor on the roster of criminals in the uncivil war.

RAP MUSICIANS HAVE IT ALL: ABUSE, SELF-ABSORPTION, TREACHERY
Luke Campbell and 2 Live Crew

LUKE CAMPBELL, SOLO RAPPER AND MEMBER OF THE GROUP 2 Live Crew, calls himself "Captain Dick." It's an appropriate nickname; Campbell talked openly in an article in the March 1993 issue of *The Source,* a magazine which covers hip-hop music and culture, about how women performed fellatio on him on stage at New York's Apollo Theater and on tour in Japan. Campbell's act and his life seem to revolve around his male organ. It's ironic that a black man today would deliberately define himself by his genitalia when black men have fought to eradicate such stereotyping since they were labelled sexual beasts during slavery. But perhaps Campbell doesn't know his history.

The performances of Campbell and 2 Live Crew have caused the group some trouble, but Campbell thrives on the controversy and is always ready to go to court to defend his First Amendment rights. 2 Live Crew's 1990 album, "As Nasty as They Wanna Be" received so many complaints from Broward County, Florida citizens that sheriff Nicholas Navarro tried to stop its sale on the grounds that it was obscene. Campbell and his Crew took the case to federal court and ultimately won a ruling from the 11th Circuit, U.S. Court of Appeals that the album did have "social value" and could not be deemed obscene. The U.S. Supreme Court let that decision stand.

Feeling vindicated, Campbell's company, Luke Records, has gone on to produce some of the most sexually graphic, hardcore rap albums on the market by his own group and others. Campbell is a hero to many for facing down those who want to censor rap lyrics and videos. He's made the world safe for raunchy, raw rap such as 2 Live Crew's "Mega Mix," which reduces women to their body parts, just as Campbell reduces himself to his penis.

Campbell's approach as a producer portrays women in only one way: as greedy, sex-driven bitches who are out to take advantage of hard-working men/rappers. The theme runs through much of rap as if it were the gospel truth. The rap "One Less Bitch," by the now disbanded rap group N.W.A. (Niggers With Attitude) sums up the way women are regarded in the genre: "To men all bitches are the same: money-hungry, scandalous groupie hoes, that's always riding on a nigga's dick/Always in a nigga's pocket." Women are generally presented as sex objects, clad in bikinis or lingerie.

Performer, producer and entrepreneur, Luke Campbell isn't at all bothered by the image he offers of blacks in his work. He is puzzled by protests from black women's groups and clergy around the country. Campbell opposes censorship of his and other rap lyrics and he likes to stress his contributions to the community. He says that his company's "money goes directly to our own, to black banks," and that he hires blacks to work in every area of his company. The father of two daughters, Campbell doesn't make any connection between the degrading way that women are portrayed in his raps with the way some young black men mistreat young black women. Money is his bottom line and he knows that the controversies over his lyrics and videos will promote sales.

Gangstas

THE OPPOSITE NUMBER OF THE DEGRADING FEMALE IMAGE IN rap is the young, tough, swaggering macho black man who carries a gun and has no qualms about using it against his enemies in the 'hood or the cops. This genre within rap is called "gangsta" rap and rappers pride themselves on their badness and bravado. Violent encounters with the police, shootouts with other black men and assaults on women are a kind of rite of passage for gangsta rappers.

Eazy-E, who helped popularize gangsta rap with N.W.A. was a former drug dealer who claimed to have fathered seven children by six different women. He died in the Spring of 1995, two weeks after announcing he had full-blown AIDS.

Public Enemy rapper Flavor Flav (real name William Drayton) was charged with attempted murder in November 1994 for allegedly firing a .380 semiautomatic gun at a neighbor he accused of having sex with his girlfriend. Flavor Flav was also jailed for 30 days in 1991 after he pleaded guilty to third-degree assault on his girlfriend.

Snoop Doggy Dogg (given name Calvin Broadus), a best-selling rapper and former gang member from Long Beach, California was arrested in Los Angeles in September 1993 on suspicion of murder; Dogg was driving a jeep when one of his bodyguards, known as Malik, allegedly shot a man named Philip Woldermariam in the back. Dogg, who served a short term on cocaine possession charges, pleaded not guilty to the murder charge.

But the rapper who seems to be trying hardest to live up to a gangsta image is Tupac Shakur. Shakur, 23, a gold-record winner was arrested in October 1993 for allegedly shooting two off-duty Atlanta police during a traffic dispute. Then in December 1993 Tupac was in the headlines again for allegedly taking part with others in an attack on a 20-year-old woman in his New York City hotel suite. Tupac's lawyers denied the charges and attorney Michael Warren characterized the woman as a "gold digger" and a groupie.

Tupac, like other rappers, has his defenders. Some see him as a victim of a long-running feud with the police because his best-selling album "2pocalypse Now" has one song with a reference to the Rodney King case that is taken to be anti-cop: "What the fuck would you do: Drop them or let them drop you? I choose droppin' the cop."

The son of two former Black Panthers, Tupac likes to boast of his outlaw heritage, saying he was in jail even as a fetus. His mother Afeni Shakur served two years in prison before being acquitted of political crimes in the 1970s and his father is still incarcerated. Tupac has the words "Thug 4 Life" tattooed on his stomach. Others point out that this is just male rapper posturing. Defenders cite the lyrics to a song Tupac co-authored called "Keep Ya Head Up," which appeals to young black women to have self-respect and perseverance and asks young men to "stop raping our women." Tupac is currently serving up to eight years for sexual assault.

PROTESTS AGAINST RAP

BLACK WOMEN HAVE ORGANIZED PROTESTS SINCE THEY HAVE been the targets of so many negative lyrics. New York City-based groups such as The Harriet Tubman/ Fannie Lou Hamer Collective, Washington, D.C.-based National Political Congress of Black Women and others held a mass rally, In Defense of Black Women & Black Culture, in July of 1993. Pressure from these groups led to an indefinite postponement of a Radio City Hall concert by gangsta rapper Dr. Dre (birth name Andre Young, Jr.).

Dr. Dre had outraged many women, and men, in the black community when he beat up Dee Barnes, hostess of a rap show on the Fox television network, in a Hollywood nightclub in January 1991. Barnes filed a $22.7 million suit against Dr. Dre and N.W.A., saying, "My lawsuit is not just about one 5-foot, 3-inch woman getting slapped around by a 6-foot, 2-inch guy. It's about how N.W.A. wages violence against women in general. Millions of little boys listen to this stuff, and they're going to grow up thinking it's all right to abuse women."

When asked about the charge, one group member explained that they were upset that Barnes had included negative comments about them from ex-member Ice Cube in a feature about the group on her rap show. Dr. Dre admitted the assault and told Rolling Stone magazine, "I just did it, you know. Ain't nothing you can do now by talking about it. Besides, it ain't no big thing—I just threw her through a door." Interestingly, there has been no report of Dr. Dre assaulting Ice Cube who is the person who allegedly made the offensive remarks.

Black women are usually seen as subservient sex objects in the world of rap music, but one popular rapper MC Lyte had a hit when she declared "Gotta get a ruffneck, a true gangsta." And rapper Yo-Yo (Yolanda Whitaker) is well-respected, and a founder of the Intelligent Black Women's Coalition which combats stereotyping of black women in rap.

In the early 1990s two female rap groups, Bitches With Problems and Hoe's Wit Attitude, decided to answer the prevailing sexism in rap music with their own blunt lyrics. Bitches With Problems's "Two Minute Brother" taunted, "Is this supposed to be good dick?/ Damn, you said you was a good lover/but you're the two-minute brother." The two female groups decided to use the same language and attitude of male rappers, but these groups quickly disappeared from the scene and males still dominate the world of rap and its images, on stage and behind the scenes.

RUSSELL SIMMONS
DEFENDS RAPPERS

RUSSELL SIMMONS, HEAD OF RUSH COMMUNICATIONS, A LEADING producer and distributor of rap music, issued a statement in support of all rap music. He said, in part: "Rap music is just that—music. It is an art form. Like all art, some is good, some is not so good. The people who make rap music are artists...Most of the time, that music is made by good people. Sometimes it's made by bad people. Always it is made by people who are products of their environment, and the environment has influenced both who they are and the kinds of music they make....These rappers...are giving voice to the thoughts and experiences of a lot of frustrated, and often misguided, youth. There has been a dangerous lack of public dialogue about the conditions in which these youth live, and the people these conditions create. To me, the problem is not gangsta rap hitting the mainstream. The problem is conditions which make gangsterism a reasonable life choice. Stifling rappers with moral outrage will not solve the real problem; killing the messenger never does....If the guardians of morality really cared about America's youth, they would not be fighting Tupac and Snoop Dogg's music. Instead, they'd fight against the conditions which led to the lives which create such music."

There are no wanted posters for the war criminals in this chapter but perhaps there ought to be. The influence, power and privilege these celebrated people possess should be used wisely. If these men and women set a high standard of respect for themselves and their community, they could be behavioral models for young people who don't have anyone to look up to.

CHAPTER SEVEN

BLACK WOMEN SPEAK

E VERYONE WHO HAS BEEN DRAWN INTO A WAR HAS A war story or two. It's no different with the Uncivil War between black women and black men. The stories from the Uncivil War are most often tales of love gone bad, relationships and marriages severed. Like all war stories, these have drama and pathos, humor and the ridiculous and the story tellers, men and women, feel they are a lot wiser for what they have been through. Some have sworn off relationships altogether, or for a time. Others have licked their wounds and rejoined the fray.

To get first person, verbatim war stories, I polled friends, colleagues and associates across the country to find women and men who would be willing to share some of the experiences they had been through or were still going through. All of the storytellers were interviewed face to face, recorded on audio tape and the tape was transcribed and edited for content. What you will read are their verbatim accounts, with only some details of their identities and that of some of the people in their stories changed to provide anonymity. Far more volunteered and were interviewed than are in this chapter on women's war stories and the following one on men's war stories. Because many of the experience were similar, not all of the stories have been included here.

I talked with both women and men in large cities around the

country because I was interested in seeing whether or not there were regional differences in how the uncivil war was being waged. I found that there is little or no difference by geographic area. Those interviewed are from Philadelphia, Detroit, Chicago, St. Louis, Oakland, New York and Cincinnati.

Most of the interviewees are employed, earning middle range incomes, and they are a mixture of married, divorced and never married, parents and non-parents. Their ages, at the time of the interviews, ranged from 19 to 57.

The most memorable stories in a war are those of the grand, epic battles that make a big difference in the final outcome of the war. But most combatants in a war are involved in smaller, more mundane daily skirmishes and confrontations. The following war stories tell of everyday, common clashes between black women and black men that created tension and fomented situations that caused them to terminate some relationships. Typically, there were underlying problems that sometimes were not addressed. But often, the final straw was something small and petty, like criticism of a particular pair of pants or the arbitrary switching of television channels when one partner was viewing another program. It may sound silly, but it's true.

Here are their real-life stories:

JACQUELINE

JACQUELINE, 43, WORKS AS AN OFFICE MANAGER IN HER NATIVE city of Chicago. She has been married and divorced four times and currently lives with her teenage son and her boyfriend, who is a graphic artist. She is also an emerging writer who has published articles in local papers and is working on a novel.

"In relationships, I've often been accused of being more of the man than the man was: I've taken care of everything, I've been the one who was leaned upon. I'm not what people expect as far as a traditional woman goes—kind of weak, kind of submissive, very dependent on a man.

"I'm not that way because I have never been convinced that that's the way a relationship should work, that by virtue of being male, a man is head of the household or runs the relationship. I always felt that a man and I were equals. Maybe, he had his area of expertise and I had mine, but no one should dominate the other.

"It irritates me when I hear a woman say 'I can't do this or I can't do that because he'll kill me.' Men generally don't say that. Or if they do, it's in jest. They're going to do what they want to do. I think that if I have to be accountable to a man—check with him or report to him—then a man should also account to a woman. I've always had a very strong sense of equality as far as male, female, black or white are concerned. If something's good for you, it's good for me. If it's bad for you, then it's bad for me.

"I always felt that way, even as a child. I don't remember being a carefree child. There were eight children in my family—six girls and two boys—and I'm the second oldest. I have always been very serious about life. Mostly, I remember observing the world rather than really being a part of it.

"I guess the first relationship I ever witnessed was the one between my mother and my biological father. He was very domineering, and she was very unhappy with it. When he came home from work, everything stopped. He was served, he was waited on. If things were not done his way, he would become physically or verbally abusive. This never seemed right to me. My parents finally separated when I was about 11 or 12 years old.

"When my mother remarried, her new husband was good as gold but she still played a subservient role. I would listen to her talk with her friends and it was standard, then, for women to be submissive. Of course, it was a different era, and women accepted it more than they do now. But I still felt that whether a woman worked outside of the home or not, it didn't mean that a man was king of everything. I just never bought into that.

"I think a lot of the way that I've dealt with my relationships has to do with how I felt about my father. I was determined that no man would dominate me the way he had my mother. But, then again, if I was able to dominate a man, I saw him as being weak and he lost his attractiveness to me. I was kind of torn; I didn't want him to be the heavy, but I didn't want to be the heavy either. I guess it comes down to finding a balance. As it turns out, I usually dealt with men who, like my father, felt that because they were male, it made them the head of the family.

"My first husband, Raymond, actually reminded me of my father. For the first couple of years (of the four we were married), he was fine. But then he started selling and using marijuana and he became abusive—physically, verbally and any other way you can think of. I would fight him back with my small fists; I wasn't going to fall into the category of abused women who moan, 'Oh, woe is me, what am I going to do now?' With me, it was an 'okay, may the best man win' kind of thing.

"But after about a year or so of that, I told myself to forget it, because it wasn't going to work. One day when he was out of the house I packed, took my kids, and left him. Leaving made me even more determined that I would never ever deal with that kind of situation again. When I filed for divorce he was upset with me—he never saw it coming—but I went ahead with it.

"My mother and women in her time took a lot from their husbands. They did whatever it took to make the marriage last—not work, but last. Longevity was what mattered. To them, it was synonymous with a happy marriage. So, a woman could say I've been married 10 years, 20 years, 30 years or whatever. But I believed that the number of years did not matter. The quality of the marriage did. Some of my mother's girlfriends would have affairs to keep the marriage together. Or their husbands would have affairs and still come home. But they weren't ideal husbands. So I grew up knowing for sure that marriage wasn't like it was in story books.

"I guess that, and a lot of other things, came into play as far as my own relationships. The one that I'm in now is probably the only long-term dating relationship I've had; all the others have been marriages. When I was coming up, it used to be that if you were dating someone and having sex with him, you had to marry him. Otherwise, you were a bad girl. I couldn't just enjoy a man, because that was naughty.

"I lived by that code for years. And I've had four husbands. It wasn't that I married bad guys. It was just that none of them was the man that I was really looking for. But I had sex with them; they were nice to me; and they had good jobs. It didn't matter whether or not I had a job or what kind of job it was. Growing up, I'd had it preached to me over and over that what mattered was to find a man with a good job.

"I remember that when I graduated from high school, I had scholarships for college, but I was not encouraged to take advantage of them. The only thing that I was encouraged to do was to go to secretarial school because it was thought that I would find a man to support me.

"I went to secretarial school for six months, graduated and married Raymond, who worked for the telephone company, making what was considered good money. I put college aside, even though I had always enjoyed school. Outside of the job, my place was in the home (not a classroom).

"I divorced Raymond after four years, and remarried two years later. My second husband, John, was an older man because, at the time, not only was a woman supposed to find a good man, but if the good, young man didn't work out, then the idea was to get a good old man. I was about 24 then, and John must have been about 41 or 42. I didn't have to work (though I did have a part time job) because he made very good money and took care of me.

"Although John was very, very good to me, he was extreme-ly possessive and always feared that a younger man would take me away from him. Our marriage was a kind of jailer-prisoner relationship. I had to account for every minute that I was away from the house, to the point where he would check the mileage on the car's odometer to see if I had traveled 25 miles when I had said I was going to see my mother, who was 20 miles away. So, even though he was good to me, he made me fearful, tense.

"I was in school at the time, and he didn't mind that. He just didn't want me to spend too much time with my studies. He would interrupt me when I was studying because he wanted my attention. After a year with him, I saw that the marriage wasn't going to work, so I left him. He filed for the divorce, but we parted on good terms.

"I met my third husband, Albert, the father of my son, on the job. He also fit everything that I'd been raised to look for: He had a good job as a pharmacist. And we were very, very good friends; we still are. But I never felt any passion for him. I loved him, but not with the kind of love that keeps you going and has you anticipating his arrival. Albert was more like the father I never had, though he was just two years older than me.

"Despite the fact that we were good buddies, I never enjoyed our sexual relations. For me, it was more about enduring sex with Albert, rather than enjoying it. A month before my 30th birthday, something happened to me that to this day I don't understand. And suddenly, I couldn't pretend anymore with Albert, I could not fake orgasms or pleasure. It became a 'Don't touch me, leave me alone.' kind of thing.

"I began to drink heavily to endure Albert's advances and I remember that once he even said, 'You always have to get liquored up for me.' And it was the only way I could really deal with sex with him. I tried to talk to him about it—to tell him what I wanted from him sexually but he wouldn't do it. Or, even if he tried, I could feel him following my instructions during the act. It was like he was asking himself, 'Did she say to the left, or to the right?' I could feel that it wasn't flowing naturally.

"Things got worse. One time, Albert presented me with a list he had kept of all the reasons I had given him for not having sex. He said that first I had been depressed because I wasn't working. Then I was overburdened because I was working. He said it was always something, always some excuse to not have sex with him.

"I looked back at my life then and thought, 'I'm almost 30

years old, and I still have not done anything I really wanted to have done.' It's like I've been living by the code of my mother and grandmothers. A code that said that 'You're a smart girl, but if you're really smart, you'll find a husband with a good job.' It was as if it was a sin, almost, to be unmarried. And if you had children, then divorced, the only way to clean that up was to get married again.

"So, I got into marriages, but they felt like death to me; I wasn't happy in them. I reached a point around this time where I thought about how I had 11-year-old twins and a newborn baby, but still had thoughts of going to college. Only, I was in a housewife mode and Albert wanted me to stay at home for at least five years to take care of our son. I couldn't do it, though. I went back to work and to school.

"At the time, I didn't really talk with anybody about how I really, really felt. I think that I was the odd woman out to many of my friends—they didn't have the same aspirations that I did. I felt frustrated, and I brought a lot of that into my relationships. It even affected the way I dealt with my daughters—I resented them after a while because I felt that not only was I blocked from what I wanted to do, but I had to see that they did what they needed to do. They were trying to come into their own, while I was belatedly trying to come into myself, so I really couldn't get as involved with them as I wanted to or needed to because it was as if we were all at the same stage.

"I was still in this unhappy third marriage when I met a guy—Alan—who was also married, but separating from his wife. We began a relationship. The sex was the best sex I'd ever had in my life. So I thought, he's got to be the one, even though there were some things about him that disturbed me. But I was overwhelmed by the sex. Plus, he was very, very much into me, attentive to me, and a wall inside me came down.

"So I divorced my third husband and married for a fourth time a couple of years later. Alan was more into our getting married than I was. He felt that was where a relationship should lead. I no longer felt I had to marry, but I lost my job and Alan was pressing for us to get married. We did, but we were never friends. I was mostly looking for sexual satisfaction, and he wanted a wife.

"But I couldn't fulfill Alan's need for constant nurturing—he was always up under me, 24 hours a day! He never tired of me; never, ever felt like 'going out with the boys.' My space has always been important to me whether I'm in love or not. There was always something kind of unsolved and unresolved going on inside me and I could deal with it best if I was alone. This was hard for Alan and other men before him to understand, and I couldn't explain it. A man has to back off and give me time to myself. I need to breathe. It's nothing against the man. It doesn't mean I don't love him, or want him, anymore. But Alan could never relate to that.

"Although our sex life was good, other things bothered me. I was in school, and Alan resented it because it took time away from him. I was also into my writing and could stay up into the wee hours writing, writing, writing. Alan would come and knock on the door of the room I was working in, and he would say, 'You're still up? You're still up? This is the time that you're suppose to be asleep.'

"Once, when I told him I was going to take a semester off, he got very excited. But then I told him it was so I could start writing a book. His response was, 'Oh, damn, then I'll never see you.' So I had to get away from him—he interfered with my writing, the only thing that I realized I ever really, really wanted to do. It got to the point where I couldn't get into him sexually, even though the sex was good. It just wasn't good enough for me to forsake my writing. After five years, I ended that marriage, too, although he didn't want us to get a divorce.

"After Alan, I decided I just couldn't do the marriage thing right. I'd had good men, I'd had good sex, I'd had the good, old man with lots of money. I had all of those things, but I still felt something was missing. I could never get anyone else to agree with me on that idea. I thought about therapy and probably would have gone if my third husband had not said that something was wrong with me, that I needed help because I did not enjoy him sexually. Even though I felt like he said that in defense of his own shortcomings, I wouldn't go to therapy after that. Actually, I always felt that if I could find one woman friend who I trusted and could open up to, she would be like a therapist.

"When I was divorced three years ago, I was scared at first because I'd always had a man to back me financially. This was the first time that I was ever completely on my own. But I was determined that I was going to stay that way. I was ready to adjust my lifestyle so that my salary would be enough to live on. And if I got involved with a man, it was not going to be because he made good money but because I just wanted him.

"I was also determined that I would have to be sexually satisfied in the relationship, and excited just by the man being home. When that kind of excitement is not there, my frustration carries over into other areas. I start going off on a man and being angry with him about things that would not ordinarily anger me because so much tension has built up inside me.

"For about a year after my divorce I didn't get involved with anybody. I would date, but nothing really serious developed. I'm not opposed to marriage, but I don't feel like I have to be married now, either. Whatever way a relationship flows is fine. If it leads to marriage, okay, if it doesn't, okay. I finally realized that every relationship doesn't have to culminate in marriage.

"One of the things I've observed is that the shortage of black men has made them think of themselves as a prize; and I think black women are at fault because they let them think that. If women were stronger, things wouldn't be that way. In my relations, I never treated men like they were the prize. I believed I was!

"Usually, when the subject of marriage comes up between a black man and woman, marriage is the man's decision—they marry if he wants to. But I don't think it should be the man's call. It's a similar thing with sex and the issue of living together. I think sex is paramount with men, and they think that if they've pleasured you, everything else is alright, and you must be satisfied. But they need to ask, to talk to women about what pleasures them. It's not their call.

"And men are all for moving in with a woman, but the idea of marriage still scares them. As I see it, if the situation warrants moving in, living together—it's the same as marriage. Black men need to think about this.

"The relationship that I'm in now is unlike any other I've had before. David is a man who has something to focus on other than me. I'm not his source of entertainment, or his everything—that's a hell of a responsibility for a woman to carry. David encourages my writing because he reads a lot and has even done some writing himself. That helps. He doesn't feel threatened or think that I'm really having an affair when I say I'm writing. And I encourage him with his art. It's not a contest between us, there's no competition. We don't try to keep each other from our work, and we've become friends. I'm myself with him without any pretense. I can bring up things that I don't like and we can discuss them, air our feelings. We might agree or disagree, but we always come back to what we really are to each other.

"This is something I haven't experienced before. I also don't feel I have to justify our having sex by saying 'I do.' I have no idea where the relationship will go, and I'm not really concerned about it. It's good now, and I hope it stays that way. I could really go on as it is right now with no problem."

DEBRA

DEBRA, 45, IS A BARBER IN OAKLAND, CALIFORNIA. SHE IS THE single mother of a daughter, 20 and a son, 13. She is currently attending college at night and plans to go into teaching.

"When I came to Oakland from a small town in Illinois in my early twenties, I was really naive and insecure; I felt threatened by male-female relationships because I thought I was inadequate—I'd always been overweight and I felt unattractive. I started out as a beautician, but I didn't feel like I was at my best as a beautician. For one thing, you're expected to compete with the other beauticians as far as your personal style and appearance. I also noticed that the women customers didn't carry on conversations about things that were really relevant.

"I switched to barbering, and because of my insecurities I tried to isolate myself from the men around me. When I worked on a customer, I made myself see only the person in my chair because I felt like everybody else was staring at my body and I didn't like that. Men actually found me sexually appealing but I didn't realize it then because I always saw myself as looking like a boy.

"I noticed that on quiet days in the barber shop, the men who came in felt comfortable getting into whatever conversation was going in, unlike in the beauty shop. I would listen intensely to their conversations and watch how men who were strangers would interact with one another. I wished that women would do that also, rather than just look at and talk about one another's clothes and hair-dos.

"The barber shop became a learning institution for me, and not only in the area of how men thought about women. The men talk about cars, about politics, and current events. The men who came into the shop always had newspapers. Before I became a barber, I never bought a newspaper, never watched the news. So being around these men at the shop opened my mind and I realized I didn't have to worry about feeling physically inadequate. I developed other interests: Some of the guys at the shop taught me how to play chess and chess became more than just a game to me. I learned that my mind could be stimulated to really think.

"Chess taught me how to pose mental challenges, but at first I used that skill to challenge men intellectually. I didn't realize I was doing that until one of the barbers pulled me to the side one day and said, 'Debra, you've got a bad habit of talking down to men.' At first I was aggravated by his comment, but then I stopped and listened to myself. I think I was-n't so much talking down to them as I was trying to get myself to the point that I could challenge a man mentally. Or maybe I was trying to make them feel insecure because I always heard them saying negative things about women and about the children that were being raised by single mothers. Their comments used to bother me.

"I can recall that when an unruly kid was acting up in the barber shop, one man said that he wished he could have that kid for about a weekend because he'd straighten him out [like the mother couldn't]. For a while, I wouldn't say anything when I heard comments like that. But then I got to the point where I felt comfortable enough to ask, 'Well, where's your son? Who's taking care of your kid?' Sometimes I felt like I was representing women in the barbershop, so I would challenge the men and what they said.

"A lot of the talk in the shop is about how men think women are in the wrong. I hear men say, 'Women don't appreciate a good man' or 'Women don't know when to shut up' or 'Women, they want too much.' When it comes to women, the conversation is always real negative.

"This kind of talk is what I used to hear from my daughter's father. He had two other children by other women and he was more of a father to them than he was to our daughter. We broke up while I was pregnant but there had never been much of a relationship anyway. I was very naive when I met him and it turns out we were very different. We never really had a friend-ship and he never helped me when she was small—just gave me money every now and then.

"Another man fathered my son, but, neither one of the two men was really the one for me. When I was younger, I think I projected what I wanted in a man on the man I was seeing or I would try and mold myself into what I thought a man wanted. I didn't accept what I really saw about them, even when I got little warning signs in the beginning of the relationships.

"One girlfriend told me she was bothered as she watched me

conform to the ways of Alfred, my son's father. He was unfeeling and had no compassion for anyone. Our relationship was one-sided: I was the giver, he was the taker. I'm a person who needs to be needed; I find it fulfilling to give myself to someone who needs me. I feel I have a lot of good to give to a man. Alfred and I eventually broke up over something petty. I had never felt comfortable telling him what I felt or thought about anything, really, but this day I looked at him and I thought his pants didn't fit him right. They were too short and made him look really stupid. I told him that, partly because I wanted to see how he was going to respond. I knew his idea was that I wasn't supposed to have any kind of input about something like this, even it was constructive criticism. He could criticize me, but I couldn't do that with him. So when I gave him my opinion, he threw a fit, acted like he wanted to blow my brains out.

"The whole thing was something very small, very minor. Another man might have simply said, 'Well, thanks Debra.' I thought I loved him because I saw him as being like my daddy, a strong man, with the ability to do things, take control of things. But when he went off on me, I knew I couldn't deal with him anymore.

"Right after I broke up with Alfred, I found out I was pregnant by him. When I called and told him, he asked me how he could know if it was his. I told him he that he knew very well that it was his and that I would have expected to hear that from a 15-year-old, not a grown man. At the time, though, I was disappointed with myself for having gotten pregnant. My daughter had just turned seven and my life was pretty stable. I had even decided to go back to school. I was really resentful with God about the pregnancy until I understood that we get hurt because we ignore the warning signs about another person. I saw the signs warning me about this man but I just didn't pay attention.

"Now, at age 44, I realize that when I do something stupid it's because I wanted to more than I didn't want to. I made a choice, and sometimes I make dumb choices. I think that in relationships we often accept less than we should because we don't discipline ourselves to be what we should be, what we want to be, what we think we ought to be.

"I think society places too much pressure on women to be married. If you aren't, people wonder if something is 'wrong' with you. I never felt insecure about not being married except for one period in my life—I was about 21 years old—when I had this feeling that I was supposed to be married. All my girl-friends who I went to school with were getting married. Now every one of them is divorced.

"Marriage is one of the best institutions in the world, I think, but I'm not looking for that at this point. I am seeing a man but it's mainly a sexual relationship, not a love thing. We have fun together but we don't put any pressure on each other about marriage.

"The thing I've come to understand about relationships is that friendship is love. Everything that draws one person to another—whether it's sexual or non-sexual, between men and women, men and men or women and women—is a type of love. And that love is content with itself. It's a good and positive thing.

"It's funny that black men don't seem to understand this. They know how to be friends with a woman, and they can be honest in that friendship. But in love relationships, they may be good men but they aren't honest with women about who they are and what they want. They just don't seem to be able to do this on a one-to-one basis with a black woman. They don't seem to know how to express their inner selves and therefore they're not really being their true, strong black selves.

"Most of the men that I work with on a patron-barber rela-tionship are really good men. They're married, and say they want a good woman in their life. But sometimes they contradict themselves in the same conversation: They'll say they have a good woman, every detail they give about her is negative. Or they say they have a good woman, but admit they don't do right by her. I wonder if they hear what they are saying.

"I had an older married man in one day who told me, 'Girl, I really got problems.' I asked him what was wrong because my customers know I'm real sensitive to what's going on in their lives. He hesitated, but then he told me he'd met a woman who he liked a lot and just couldn't leave alone. I asked about his wife and he called her a good wife who he wouldn't leave her for this other woman. He also said he didn't trust the woman. I told him he didn't really have a dilemma and that I didn't feel sorry for him. As I saw it, he could take a chance and lose his wife, a good woman and a good wife, and wind up with somebody who he didn't trust. That's the kind of situation that just blows my mind.

"Another guy who's married and from a well-established family came in and we were talking about marriage and sex. He said that if it wasn't for society's standards, he probably never would have gotten married. He told me that if he had to depend on his wife alone for sex, he would probably never be happy. He had always had 'outside' women from the time he got married. We're friends and I know his wife and know how he treats her, so I asked him, 'Why do you have to be so ugly with your wife sometimes?' He said he did it just to raise hell. 'That's just the way I am,' he told me.

"Even though this man felt at a certain point that it was time for him to have a good woman in his life, marriage didn't mean settling down in his mind. The main complaint he had about his wife was that she only wanted sex once a month. I told him that he needed to talk to her because they'd obviously had a good sexual relationship before they were married. But he told me they hadn't, that the situation was the same before they married. Since he had married her anyway, it seemed to me that he just had to accept her as she was. And I told him so. The things he told me are the kind of thing that just lays me out. I really can't figure men out sometimes.

"Or women either. A friend of mine told me a while back that he thought one of the problems with women is that they say they want a good man, and they can list the positive things they want, starting with: He has to be good looking, and he has to make a certain amount of money. But my friend wondered what women were offering in a relationship. Men and women demand a lot from the other person, but I realize that the positive things we're looking for in another person are often the things we really want to improve in ourselves. And often the things we don't like in another person are things that we haven't disciplined about ourselves.

"If I was going to describe the kind of long-term relationship I wanted, I'd have to say that I want a relationship where I am secure about the love, like the love I share with my granddaughter. It's just there. I don't have to question it.

"I also need a relationship where there's understanding. Without understanding there is no compromise, there is no acceptance, there is no forgiveness. I'd like a man who is stronger, more determined than I am, someone who will help me with my weaknesses and inspire me.

"I would like to have friendship and a lot of interacting in a relationship. I want the two of us to be able to talk at the end of the day and share the things that have happened to each of us—what we've seen and learned. I think that a male-female relationship should be one of the greatest things in the world. Men need women and women need men. We can teach each other. I know I've grown from each of the relationships I've been in.

"In my relationships, it's also important to me that a man knows and believes in God. That way, he'll have a sense of direction and will be in touch with his spiritual side. I believe there's a spiritual part in all of us that cries out to be shared. Black women seem willing to tap into it, but black men aren't. I think that's one reason black relationships don't work—there is no spiritual sharing. Black men and women would get along better if we could learn to stimulate each other spiritually."

PAULA

PAULA, 37, WORKS FOR A FEDERAL GOVERNMENT AGENCY IN

her home town of Philadelphia. She is single and has never been married.

"I didn't have any boyfriend-girlfriend relationships when I was in high school because my mother passed away around the time I began high school and I had to concentrate on just growing up without her. So it wasn't until I got to college that my eyes were opened up, personally, to sex and male-female relationships.

"The college I attended was a state school and, in addition to the men on campus, there was a military base ten miles away. So both groups of men competed for the affections of the women at the school. But, the military guys had the money to wine and dine us, plus they had cars. The guys on campus could only compete by saying, 'Baby I love you,' or 'I'm the one. I'm smart. I have it all.' So, I dated a guy from the base and one from school.

"But there was a feeling in general that these college relationships were short-term. It was socially accepted to date one guy for five or six months, then move on to another guy. That went on all the time on campus.

"In my freshman year I started dating a guy from the military, an older man, who was married, though his wife wasn't there with him. Now, my grandparents raised me after my mother died, and they didn't tell me anything about sex. And since I didn't date in high school, I wanted to know and experience everything by the time I got to college. This man taught me a lot, but the horrible thing was that I fell in love with him. Since he was married, our relationship couldn't go any further and I moved on to someone else.

"For the rest of the three years I went to college, I was in and out of many, many relationships. It wasn't until I left school that I started settling on one man and after that I had a couple of good relationships. The one that lasted the longest while I was a student was with a guy from New York. We even lived together my last year and talked about marriage, but we never got into actually planning it.

"After graduation, I decided to move to Chicago to work, and I met a man, Tyrone, who I dated for all of the three years I lived there. He was from Trinidad, and he showed me a lot about what a woman should expect from a man. Tyrone always brought something with him when he knocked on the door, either a flower, a pizza pie or a bottle of wine. During my time with him, I became used to having a man treat me with respect, put me on a pedestal and show me kindness. I thought that was how relationships really were.

"Our relationship ended because Tyrone was homesick and decided to go back home. I was also homesick and, in the beginning, he and I had kind of latched on to each other as two people both pining for home. I considered going to Trinidad with him, but I was scared to venture that far. When Tyrone left, I was heartbroken and after six months I moved back to Philadelphia. I had gotten used to Tyrone and the way he treated me. But as far as men go, I got a rude awakening when I got back to Philly.

"Arnold, the first boyfriend I had after I got back, had just been divorced and was still hurting. We met at a bar and later started going out. Like the married military man I dated in college, Arnold wined and dined me because he had categorized me as the type of woman you had to treat like that. I thought he was the best thing that ever happened to me: he would send flowers to me at work, he cooked for me, fed me, and was a good companion. That special treatment and pampering lasted for a couple of years—until he had my heart—then it stopped. Because I was in love, I did a lot to keep our relationship going. But I came to see that what Arnold really wanted was to control me.

"I remember one day when he was at my house, I was watching the television show 'Knots Landing.' Now, I was a 'Knots Landing' fool, but he didn't like me to watch the night time soaps. He said, 'You shouldn't be watching this,' and got up and turned to the Public Broadcasting Service (PBS) channel. I'll never forget it. The PBS program was just a bunch of old men sitting around a table talking.

"Arnold and I were sitting on the sofa and he had his arm around me, but I was miserable and thinking about how I was missing 'Knots Landing.' So I got up, went into my bedroom and turned on the television in there. Of course, Arnold got pissed off and left my house.

"But I understood the psychological thing that was happening between us. He was trying to control the relationship between us. And I was trying to hold on to him. But I wouldn't let the fact that I wanted him prevent me from doing what I really wanted to do.

"That television incident was a turning point where I decided I wasn't going to be that unhappy in that relationship or any other one again. I was going to have to be able to do what I liked. And a man was going to have to accept me for the things that I did that he might not like, whether it's watching soap operas or anything else.

"After that, the only good times Arnold and I had together were when we'd go to church together. But after church, things were dull. He'd come to my house and cook for me but he would always buy groceries and insist that those were the kinds of foods I should have in my refrigerator when he came over. He also said that the way he cooked was the way I should eat. Again, because I was in love, I did what he wanted me to, but I knew I had to stop behaving like that.

"I was being torn apart because I didn't know how to break up with him. I just knew I didn't want to be controlled that way anymore. As long as I was faking it, going along with him, everything was okay. But I didn't want to fake it anymore.

"While I was going through these feelings, I had an automobile accident as I was driving alone one Saturday night. They took me straight to the hospital, and I asked an aunt of mine to call Arnold and tell him about the accident. She did, but he never came to visit. I had surgery that Monday and I stayed in the hospital until that Saturday.

"Arnold called only once and that was to tell me why he couldn't come to see me. He said he couldn't handle it, that he was going through some heavy things, too. I thought that was a bad way for him to react. In a way, I was kind of glad he did because it made me focus on my recovery. I had my mouth wired and couldn't talk or eat. I had to concentrate on getting well, and while I was doing that, I was also breaking away from him. That was the only good thing about my accident. When I was back on my feet, he wanted to come back and I said no at first, then relented and saw him a couple of times for dinner. But it wasn't the same and the relationship ended.

"For the next couple of years I pretty much stayed away from men. I didn't want to give years to a relationship and have it not work out. Instead, I went back to school and started focusing on my career. It paid off because I got promoted and started to excel on my job. I moved into a better place, and bought better furniture. I was doing okay by myself.

"Then, when I was thirty, I met Calvin, another older man (he was 16 years older than me) who was very nice. I had decided by then that I wanted a meaningful relationship. Calvin didn't really fit in with my lifestyle or friends, and he didn't really want to. Our relationship involved just the two of us. He liked doing things for me without wanting to control me. He didn't know a lot about women when we met, but I taught him a lot in the seven years we were together. We got along well because we communicated with each other. I could tell him how I felt about things and he shared with me how he felt. The relationship was good for me because I always had someone to lean on, someone to talk to who understood me. Calvin moved out-of-state for his job two years ago, but we're still friends and I saw him when he was in town a few weeks ago.

"I had concentrated on Calvin only for the first couple of years that we saw each other, and he was the only one that I slept with. But I did date other guys. My situation sort of calls to mind Spike Lee's movie *She's Gotta Have It.*

"I was also going out with Sonny, Evan and Bernard. Sonny was kind of far out. My friends said 'crazy,' but he was the most fun. He had a Porsche and we'd drive to the country with the top down and have picnics. Women liked him and spoiled him, so I had to deal with that.

"Evan was a straight-arrow guy who always wore a tie. We'd go to all the black plays and to the annual Ebony Fashion Fair. Evan showed me off around his big-time politician friends and I'd always dress my best and just have a good time. But Evan also did a couple of things that stopped me in my tracks. He asked me to pick him up at the airport once when he was returning from a business trip. I had put my nice table cloth on the table, had the candles lit and was ready for him to come over to my house.

"I'd been thinking that since he'd been gone a few days and hadn't seen me, we would spend a nice evening together. Wrong. I was standing there waiting when he came off the plane, but all he wanted to do was go home to his house. He told me he was pretty tired, so I dropped him off at his place, but all I could think about was how I had spent my whole day getting prepared for the evening—cleaned my house, used my gas to drive to the airport, met him at the gate—and there he was, tired. I was mad then, but I can laugh about it now.

"Bernard, the third guy I was also dating, had a lot of other women because he was handsome. We were good friends and he was nice to me, but neither of us ever wanted to commit to each other. It seems he didn't want to be attached to just one lady. As far as I knew, he had had a girlfriend at one time and after they broke up, he never saw another woman for a long stretch.

"But he was always there for me until I met someone else and it got serious. I'd drop Bernard like a hot potato until my new relationship was over, then I'd pick him back up. I could pick up the phone and call him, and he'd say, 'Hey, okay, let's go do something.' So I was never lonely between my serious relationships.

"The problem Bernard and I had, though, was that he wanted me to depend on him. That was hard because I had been taking care of myself for a long time. But I would call him when I had trouble with my car, and he would work on it, doing whatever was needed. That helped keep our relationship going, but things changed when I went back to school.

"Bernard would come over and watch television while I studied; I was paying a lot of money for school so I had to study hard. Because Bernard had never gone to college he didn't understand that. He came over once to watch a basketball game with me, but I was at the dining room table studying and couldn't stop to join him. After that incident, Bernard stopped coming around.

"I basically had good relationships with these men: Sonny, Evan and Bernard, but didn't want to be attached to any of them. I never once considered marrying any of them, especially after I watched so many of my friends' relationships and marriages fall apart.

"I met yet another man on a blind date. Harold was a nice guy who was quite a bit older, in fact, he was close to retirement. He asked me out to dinner for our first date, and we went to a very good restaurant and had a great meal and really good conversation. Afterwards, Harold invited me to his house for a drink since he lived nearby. We got into his car and as we pulled into his sub-division, I noticed a car pull up behind us. I asked if someone was following us and he just said it appeared so— that's all he said. We drove on and as he pulled into his driveway another car pulled up behind us.

"Harold asked me to wait in the car while he got out. I thought it was maybe one of his buddies who had spotted him. But suddenly I heard shouting back and forth and the next thing I knew, a woman was at the window asking me who I was. Harold made her get in her car and leave, and we went into his house. By this time I really needed a drink. So did he.

"About fifteen minutes after we were inside, the phone rang. Of course it was the same woman and after Harold got her off the phone I asked him what was going on with her. He told me that she had lived with him up until a month before, and she thought that I was the woman who had caused them to break up, though the breakup was his decision, not the fault of another woman. The whole thing seemed like a 'fatal attraction' to me and I asked him to get me out of his house before she came back again.

He took me home and said, when we parted, 'I hope this won't jeopardize my chance to see you again.' Of course I never, ever saw him again though we did speak on the phone. But a male friend warned me that being with Harold could put me in a dangerous situation, so I dropped him.

"I've tried to figure out why men are like they are and I can't. A lot of black men do things just to see how much you'll put up with from them. And in my early relationships when the guy ended the relationship, I wondered what I'd done; why they didn't like me; if my body was the problem. Or was it that they just wanted to have sex? Later, I decided 'no,' I wasn't the problem; it's just that black men do some stupid shit in relationships, like the things I've experienced. And a lot of black women are bitter because of it. I went through some pain with my first boyfriend and other men I saw in college. But when I hit 30, I told myself men were going to treat me differently; I wasn't going to go through crazy stuff with them anymore.

"A main problem I've had with black men is in their wanting to control me. I think that it's because they're intimidated by my accomplishments and ability to manage. But the one thing I don't want is to be controlled. And I'm not. That's why I'm not bitter. A man has to take me the way I am or leave me alone.

"I think another key reason I'm not bitter is that I've never allowed anybody to give me anything. Everything I own, I bought. Everything that I wear, I bought. I've had diamond earrings and pearls. In return, I've never given expensive gifts, big items. Some women buy men a lot of things and then when the relationship breaks up they're angry. They spend maybe two or three hundred dollars to buy a man, say, a piece of jewelry, and then they find another woman wearing it. I'd be mad, too. I'd be bitter. I'd be ready to kill both of them. That's why I've never done that. So there's no bitterness.

"Don't misunderstand me. I've had the pain that the end of a relationship brings. After I broke up with one man I went home that Friday with a nice bottle of wine. I turned off all my lights and lit some candles and turned on some soft music. I sat right there and got drunk. When I woke up the next day I was still feeling the pain. Plus, I had a hangover. What I did was: took the phone off the hook, lit the candles again and stayed at home all day. I drank more wine and didn't talk to anybody. That was Saturday, the second day.

"Sunday came and I asked myself, do I still feel the pain? Well, it was going away. This is working, I thought. By Monday morning when I went back to work, I was fine. If it happens again, I'll just say, here comes some pain, and I'll know what to do. It worked for me!

"Right now, I'm content and I'm not looking for a relationship at all. Friends of mine in relationships are breaking up all around me. They're miserable, and I'd rather be single than be in a marriage where I'm miserable. I have an aunt who's been married 45 years, and she says, 'Either you have a man or you don't. If you have one, you'll put up with some shit.' That rings true to me. I think my relationships will be better from here on because I know now that there will be some shit. If somebody comes along, fine, but I'm not the type of woman who has to have a man to be fulfilled. I know there's good and bad in every male-female relationship. I want one that will be meaningful, one where the man thinks of me as an asset, a woman who has a lot to offer."

ELAINE

ELAINE, 49, WAS BORN AND RAISED IN PHILADELPHIA AND LIVES in Cincinnati. She owns and operates a real estate firm and gives some of her free time to working with young people. A mother of five adult children, she was married for sixteen years before her divorce in 1977.

"I started my real estate business at the same time that I began divorce proceedings. At first I did residential and commercial real estate brokerage. But I've always been one who believed in looking for what is not being done; if a person is going into business she needs to be an exception not the rule, otherwise she won't get anywhere with it. There were no blacks in Cincinnati involved in real estate development to any significant extent when I was starting out. So it made sense to me to go into this area.

"Even as a newcomer to business, I understood the importance of networking and aligning myself with those who were powerful enough to assist me in moving forward. That's what I did. Interestingly, most of the contacts I made were not in Cincinnati. It was hard getting off the ground, but through my contacts I got a contract to build a suburban housing complex and another to manage one of the largest black-owned office building in the city.

"A lot of the black men I dealt with felt that I was too strong, too aggressive and they couldn't handle that. But I was raised to be all that I could be, and not to be subjected to, or tolerate, anything that was wrong. Folks used to say that I put up with a lot of negative stuff in my marriage. And, yes, I did, but it was like the old joke that says there was a little boy who grew up not talking. His parents couldn't figure out what was wrong with him because he was normal in every other way. One day they took him to a specialist, but he couldn't figure out what was wrong either. At dinner one night, the boy's mother served soup, and he looked up and said, "The soup's cold." His mother and the whole house were very excited and finally somebody asked the boy why he had never said anything up until then. He answered that up until then, everything had been fine.

"That's how my marriage was. As long as everything was fine, I didn't mind being submissive, being a traditional wife.

Actually, I enjoyed it because I knew that I was capable of stepping up and making aggressive decisions when it was necessary. I had supported my husband in his business and in our marriage for a number of years. And when the marriage was over I knew I would be able to keep on going.

"I know that I'm intelligent and don't have to tolerate anything I don't want to in relationships, but I enjoy letting a man take the lead; I have no problems with that as long as I trust and respect him. If I don't, if the trust or respect are in question, it's time for me to take charge and do what I have to do. I realize that men, for the most part, do not expect a woman to do that. They expect her to play games. And I suppose that women assist them in that belief because we play games, too.

"Now, I do play games when I'm working because I'm negotiating situations that will lead me to the next goal. But the problem for me is that I don't want to play games in my personal life. And I don't want to have to do guess work. I'm very literal. If I say something is black, it is black. If I say something is white, it's white. And that's how I am in a relationship, too—yes means yes, and no means no. I don't appreciate a man coming back to me later and saying, "I didn't know you really meant that." That's game playing, and our whole culture is programmed to play games. Black people have adjusted to that, but I just can't do it. I need a literal translation of anything that's being said. I don't need the game.

"After my divorce I had a real awakening going into the single world again, after so many years. I was very naive about male-female relationships, but I learned a lot quickly. Meeting men was not a problem. I'm a fairly outgoing individual and I enjoy interacting with people. And I try to avoid always being in the same circle of friends. That comes from being in the business world where, after working with one circle of people, I have to find new ones to do business with so as not to become stagnant.

"So I was always out there meeting people, especially men. And I learned early that simply because you meet a man doesn't make the encounter something important. There were many men who I had to leave alone. And others who I went out with were, for the most part, intimidated by me. The thing is that, as a woman in business, I learned to recognize quality; that's how I made decisions about who I would do business with in the first place. Making those kinds of decisions, I also learned to recognize those men who are quality individuals in my personal life.

"The trouble with our African American men is that they don't recognize that they are quality individuals. I used to say I'm not raising [a man who is] some other mother's child. But that's about what it adds up to with African-American men; a black woman is expected to raise them or teach them the things they haven't grasped, especially about relationships.

"I had my children to teach and I raised them. I don't need to teach grown men. I need a man who has some understanding of his own value and worth, someone who carries himself with the dignity that comes with this understanding. I have this understanding, and it can be a problem. If a person knows who she is, it's difficult for a man who doesn't know who he is to feel comfortable around her.

"African American women are faced with a predicament when it comes to black men who expect women to take a back seat to them. But it's one thing to respect a man and allow him to lead. It's another thing to take a back seat to someone who does not know how to lead.

"If a woman can lead, she doesn't mind allowing a man to take that lead. But he's got to know what he's doing. On the other hand, some men have the ability, talent and other qualities you need to lead, but they don't appreciate that they have these gifts.

"I was in a relationship with a man like that. This brother was, and still is, a beautiful man. There was good chemistry between us and the relationship was going well, I thought, but one day he said, "This can't go on. We have to stop seeing each other." When I asked why, he said, "It's because you are too strong. I know that you are going to do great things and I cannot. I will feel very intimidated by that and at some point it will reflect on how I react to you. And that's not a healthy thing for me."

"So we split up, but we've remained very dear friends through the years. I told him that he was extremely gifted and I wouldn't be attracted to somebody who had nothing to offer. In those days he was in sales, and I suggested he move from sales and get involved with administration because he might find he was good at it. I could see him surpassing anybody else in the field. He was attempting to follow a younger brother he had who was an exceptional salesman. And he just wasn't geared to sales. He would take it too hard if he didn't win a contract he'd gone after. Today, he owns his own business and is very successful. And will tell anyone in a minute that he owes all of that success to me. But at the time we broke up, he just didn't understand how gifted he was.

"I've seen more men in that mode, than not, and past a certain point, I reached a stage where I became a bit hardened to it. So when somebody says, "I just can't live up to you," I say, "No problem" and keep on going. It doesn't phase me anymore.

"It's important for women to learn to appreciate themselves and let that be sufficient enough so that a man is not a necessary part of their lives. Women are more than capable of survival without men, but if we are involved with men, they should enrich our lives. I think that the saddest aspect of brothers and sisters trying to work together is the failure of men to realize that the women do not want to overshadow them, but simply to complement them and be complemented by them. When women understand that they can move on if a relationship is not working, they'll be able to identify a solid relationship. We've just got to go past a whole lot of folks to get to it!

"In looking for relationships, it's not enough to simply identify someone who is handsome and has money or has a good job. I've learned we need to look at people almost in a business sense and assess whether or not a person is going to be a healthy partner. Of course, I don't rule out the emotional side. I couldn't marry anybody whom I didn't love. I also wouldn't marry somebody I loved who didn't fit into my world—I don't really think that I could love somebody who didn't. And I would have to fit into his.

"I never believed that I had to be married just for the sake of being married. But I firmly believe that there are people who are perfect for each other. If that person doesn't come along, settling for anything less than that perfect person, is absolutely not going to work. At least it won't work for me. I don't think that means that a man has to be in a specific field or profession. I had an aunt who was a nuclear physicist who married a custodian, and their marriage lasted until her death. It was the most beautiful, positive relationship I've ever seen. Neither of them compromised on the quality of person they wanted.

"I have a problem with African-American men not recognizing women's intelligence. If a man is handsome, he assumes that any female he meets wants him. If they're in a good financial position, they also assume that they're in great demand. But no matter how much in demand a man is, he should at least give a woman credit for having some common sense—don't give her a line that's impossible to buy. And our men will do that. For instance, a federal employee once told me that he couldn't make a date we had scheduled because he had a meeting to attend at work. I knew that in his capacity there were no evening meetings. But I didn't argue. I thought, that's fine. You make your meeting, I'm making my life.

"It's an issue when black women are aggressive, when they take the lead. We're not supposed to do this—the man is supposed to. But I took care of my children. Nobody else raised them. I took care of running a business. Nobody else did that. When that business was down, I had to deal with it. When it was up, I had to deal with it. Whatever went on with the children and their lives, I had to deal with that. There wasn't any man who was going to step in after my divorce and take that on.

My children were not any man's responsibility. They were mine. My business was my responsibility. It was my dream. It fulfilled my goals, my aspirations. So how could someone else step in and tell me what to do or lead me?

"It used to be that in relationships I couldn't talk to a man about what I was doing because he'd think he was supposed to interject something that would be helpful and I would be thrilled and happy forever that he had given me the answer to the problems of the world. But no man expected me to have answers for what was going on in his business. Men expect a woman to listen, attentively or sympathetically while they go ahead and do what they have to do.

"This chauvinist attitude prevails in business dealings, too. I had to deal with contractors on a 3 1/2 million dollar project who used to call me 'honey.' But I learned how to deal with them. I flipped it right back at them. It didn't have to happen but once or twice. I called them 'honey' a couple of times, and they got the message. But in relationships it was more difficult.

"When I think about the kind of man who would be healthy for me, I know that he has to have the same aspirations, the same dreams that I have. I also want him to have the same kind of commitment to our people that I have—that's paramount for me. But I also don't necessarily think that opposites attract; I think a person doesn't love herself very much if she wants somebody who's just the opposite of her. I happen to love me a lot and as a result of that I want somebody just like me. I'm comfortable with me and I'll be just doubly comfortable with somebody else who's like me. I know that will work."

CHAPTER EIGHT

THE MEN SPEAK

S EVERAL MEN ACROSS THE UNITED STATES ALSO SHARED their experiences of courtship, love and marriage openly and honestly. The men who were interviewed in New York City, St. Louis, Oakland, and Chicago were, for the most part, employed full-time, earning middle-class incomes. The common thread running through their true stories is a desire for strong, stable, positive relationships and friendships with black women.

Each man was interviewed in person in 1993, and a transcript of the entire interview was edited for space. As with the women, the men whose stories follow came to be interviewed through personal and professional contacts of the author.

JIMMY

JIMMY, 42, WAS BORN IN MISSISSIPPI, BUT GREW UP IN CHICAGO, where he still lives with his wife and two children. He works for an express mail service and devotes much of his spare time to local groups that are working with black youth. He is also pursuing his own study of African and African American history, culture and philosophy.

In the interview, Jimmy spoke about the impact that his service in the Vietnam War had on his relationships and his marriages. He also talked about coming to terms with his father and with himself. His story:

"I've been married three times. The first marriage was to my high school sweetheart, Andrea. I was eighteen, she was seventeen. What happened was that I went to live with an aunt in Texas at one point when I was in high school because I got into some trouble with Chicago gangs. Although Andrea stayed in Chicago, I didn't want to go back, so I eventually joined the Navy. When I got out of basic training, I did go back to Chicago briefly and Andrea and I got married because she was pregnant.

"When I got out of the service in December 1970, we tried to start a life together, but I had gotten into using drugs and drinking during the war and our marriage only lasted a year and a half after I got back. My eldest daughter is from that marriage.

"I wound up going back home to live with my mom, but at the time, I was into drinking and drugging because of my experiences in Vietnam. Over there, I was on river patrol, going up and down the Saigon River to give fire support to land troops. In the year and seven months that I was there, I only had one home leave of 30 days. I got out of the service because I got into some trouble over some fighting and drugs and drinking and wound up being sent to Hawaii for a court martial. In the end, I got out of the navy with an honorable discharge.

"When I got back home, it was hard trying to readjust and find a job. Over in 'Nam' I found a unity among black people—the brothers in the service—that I've never found here. The brothers would die for each other there. If we had that kind of unity here, no one could put us in the situation that we're in today. So it had a big effect on me, coming back and seeing people doing the same thing that they were doing when I left, or doing even worse. I didn't want to go to school then, but Andrea was going to Roosevelt University to try and get a degree; she was more the 'brain person' than I was. I kind of envied her for being able to go to a university.

"I talked to her about a lot of things that had happened to me in the service, but there were a lot of things that I couldn't share until after I went to treatment. What I needed to do was go into a rehabilitation program. Andrea and I eventually separated and I found another lady who I fathered another child by. But my drinking and drugging got in the way of that relationship—alcohol and drugs became more important for me than family life. All I wanted to do was get out there and party and do the things that everybody else I knew was doing, instead of really being the responsible man that I was supposed to be. I also got involved with a few other women at this time.

"It went on like that for about ten years—from the time I got out of the service at 20, until I was 30 years old and went into treatment at a 28-day program at Westside Veterans Administration Hospital in Chicago.

"It's been 11 years since I've had a drink or drugs. It's been rough learning how to grow up because I first used drugs and drink when I was a kid. I came up in a life where that's all everyone did—partying was the thing. And my father was an alcoholic. It was 20 years yesterday that he died from hemorrhaging in the brain. He was found in a room where he had been drinking. Thinking about my father yesterday, I wound up facing some realities about myself. I knew there were some wounds that I hadn't healed and I cried—I hadn't acknowledged until my father died that I did love him, even though he was the way he was. I didn't ask for him as a father, but he was who God gave me. He had his good side and his bad. And he did the best that he could with what he had.

"His own father was an alcoholic who beat his wife. Then, my father did the same thing with my mother. This violence was in our lives, like a revolving door, and I knew the cycle had to be broken. When I went through treatment and got married this last time, I told myself it wouldn't be the way it had been in my past. Through treatment, I learned a lot about myself—that I was a self-centered little mamma's boy who liked for people, especially women, to cater to me. If they didn't, I'd get angry. They were supposed to do what I wanted them to do. That little kid in me who never grew up, wanted things his way. And I had to face that part of myself and start learning how to 'be a man.'

"I realized after my father died, that I still didn't know how to be a man, or how to be a role model someone could pattern their life after. It's an experience I'm going through now—trying to learn to be a man to my son. I know that I don't want it to be like my father was for me, or the way I've been with the daughters I've fathered. With them, I was more or less just a sperm donor, not a father. I give them material things and money, but I didn't know how to give them love or myself. After I went into treatment and started working on becoming the best person that I could be, I went to them and asked if I could be their friend.

"I'm not an easy person to live with but in my present marriage, I've found a friend, a woman who I can share my deepest secrets with. And she shares her deepest secrets with me. We met on the job and we've been married for seven years; we've learned to be able to let each other be who we are. We have our differences—she's a Jehovah's Witness and I'm not; and I like spending money, whereas she likes to save and plan and do things. But even with our differences, we're able to keep our relationship going.

"We have a daughter, four, and a son, who's 19 months old. My wife works one or two days a week for the same company where we met, but I wanted her to stay home and take care of the kids. I know what it was like staying with this person and that person when you're growing up. And I think it's better for her to raise our children because I've learned that the first five years in a child's life are a time of bonding, a time when they form whoever they're going to be.

"In order for her to stay home, we had to lose our house, but it's turned out for the best. It wasn't worth going through that struggle of us both working around the clock, trying to live a fabulous life that was making us miserable. So we moved into an apartment. We're closer knit, now, because we're right there together.

"And, too, my wife has been able to work on herself and see a lot of things about her past that she's shared with me; and I've shared some things that happened with me and my childhood. I've had to deal with these issues and face the monster inside, the one you live with but try to stuff down and say is not there, but he really is. I've had to face him and heal the child within.

"I went through the Alcoholics Anonymous 12-step program, and there's a step which says you have to take moral inventory of yourself. That means you have to take a butt-naked look and see just who you really are. Your assets and your liabilities. When I first started out, I could have made a list long as I was tall on the bad things that I knew about myself. I didn't know any good things. But with time, and God's help, I learned that I do have some good qualities. Like a priest said, "God don't make junk."

"I believe I have a reason for being here and part of it is learning to do His will and not mine. That was really hard because me being a self-centered mamma's boy, I wanted to do things my way. But God has a thing called pain and pain can be either a motivator or it can kill you. I tried to get rid of my pain by drinking and drugging. I even attempted suicide. So I've learned to use the pain as a motivator, something to help me grow up. Through each pain, I've learned something, then I've moved on from there. I know that He's not going to give me more than I can bear in a day.

"I read recently that my name in West Africa is Kwame, born on a Saturday. When I read it, it was like, wow, this is me! It really got me going to find out who I was because I had looked for so long. I'd been wearing so many different hats—trying to be this, trying to be that: a playboy, a drug dealer, a pimp. I'd played all these games but never really knew who I was. It was not until I got to be 30 years old that I began to learn who Kwame was. And I had to go inside to find out. It's been some experience, but it's worth it because God, as I understand Him, is helping me. I believe nothing happens in this world by mistake. He doesn't make a mistake, and I had to go through all that I did to get to be where I'm at now.

"As for my son, I'm teaching him to respect and love a woman for who she is. And I want him to love God, to love himself as an African man and to love his people. And if he can do these things, if I can even get these things into him, then he has a chance to make it."

MARCUS

MARCUS, 30, WAS BORN AND RAISED IN BROOKLYN, THE YOUNGEST of seven children in a two-parent home. He attended public grade schools, went to a private high school and then to Georgia Institute of Technology in Atlanta. At the time of the interview he had been married for a month.

"After I graduated, I returned to Brooklyn. When I came back I dated one woman for three years. That relationship didn't work out because we just couldn't overcome certain differences. My wife and I also have differences, but they don't prevent us from having a very productive and growing relationship.

"The woman I was involved with earlier—her name was Joan—was the youngest of four children in her family. She didn't have a lot of vision as far as her goals. She was very supportive of mine—I think she would have backed whatever I strived to be. But a lot of times, that wasn't enough for me.

"A lot of people like a relationship where the other person is totally dependent on them, where they're the focal point of the whole relationship. But when it's that lopsided, it doesn't tend to work out. I believe you need more of a partnership, as opposed to just one person being the total focus. That was the main reason why it didn't work out between me and Joan. I think there would have been a time where I was striving to achieve certain goals—financial, personal, spiritual or whatever—and I would have needed someone who would actively participate in those goals instead of staying behind in the shadows. Joan loved me. But she was lacking in vision for herself even though she had a college degree in hospital administration. But she had no vision beyond what I wanted in life.

"I need someone to criticize me, as well as support me, to give me a different perspective because no one can look at a situation completely objectively all the time, especially a black man or black woman. I think in today's society, with different stresses coming from the work place, and from society in general, it's essential that each person bring a different perspective to a relationship. Black men and women can come together as one, but can be two entities at the same time.

"Joan and I talked about this several times and she understood, but she just didn't know what it meant to have a personal goal outside of what someone else wanted her for her, whether it was her mother, her older sister or whoever. She just didn't know how to set goals.

"I don't want to stereotype and say that this is the way black women are—like Joan. I think you'll see this kind of thing in black and white women. Of course, you can also see black women who are very aggressive and who do have a lot of vision. A lot of older black women had a tremendous vision but were unable to do anything about it because someone—either a husband, mate or society in general—held them back.

"Black people have always had vision. I think. We couldn't have survived as long as we have without having some type of vision. But it's one thing to have a vision, another thing to get someone else to see it, and another thing to know how to go about achieving that goal.

"With Joan, it finally got to the point where I told her that I cared about her, I loved her from the bottom of my heart, but...How do you tell someone that you've been with for three and a half years, someone that you care about, that you want to end the relationship, especially after you've talked about marriage? Can you do it without having a definite reason, other than that the two of you have a difference in vision?

"It would have been different if there was someone else involved. And she hadn't done anything to offend me. It was just that she wasn't the type of person I was looking for, a person who could help rear my children, someone who I could definitely depend on on the home front if I was not there. What if something happened to me and we had children—if I died, for instance? Would she have been able to carry on? A lot of people don't get to a point where they can do things on their own unless they're forced to. Based on our relationship and the way it had developed over the years, I felt that this is how Joan was; she would never have done certain things unless she was forced to.

"So I told her, "I love you, but I think the best thing for you is for us to break off. Maybe then you will be forced to regroup and start to strive for your own personal goals. I think it would be better for both of us in the long run if we broke it off." And so we parted.

"The woman I married had a lot of vision on her own when we met. She didn't see things the same way as I did. And she doesn't agree with something just because I was the one who presented it. She disagreed with me on things. She challenged me, challenged me to prove myself right. We're both Christians, so we share a lot of the same views. But she's forced me to take another look at myself.

"I've seen older people who are locked into a certain mind set. That's because of the way they've been taught—they've never come across anything that challenged their mind-set. And when you try to show them a different perspective, they're totally against it. I think that you need someone to challenge you and present another view. It can help you grow.

"There's a definite struggle going on between black men and women, not so much because of tangible things, but because of their perceptions. For instance, a lot of black women say that black men are going for white women; and they have a lot of different philosophies about why. They say there's something about a successful black man that attracts him to a white woman. Or, in order for him to be successful, he has to be with a white woman. I don't think that's true. I never had a desire to marry a white woman—I just didn't think a white woman could give me the things that I wanted as a black man. There's a perception that you see a lot of black men in the public eye with white women or women of other races (as compared to black women with white men). This is true if you look at some black entertainers, athletes, politicians, men who are in the public eye. They give the perception that when a black man makes it, he gets a white woman.

"Today, a lot of black women are also going for white men. I think a black woman might marry a white man because she feels that a black man can't do the same things for her in society that a white man can. To me, her perception is screwed up. Black women who date white men and black men who date white women are making very strong negative statements, not only about themselves, but about the black race. I think they really need to look at where their minds are.

"Society has forced black people into a certain mold. We have a lack of respect for each other as individuals—black men have very little respect for black women and vice versa. I see it even with the high school students who I work with in a special small business program. I think a lot of this disrespect stems from the family unit. Black people need to work on some of the things that are causing bad relationships between men and women. As a Christian, I think we need to grab the strength that comes from walking in a Christian life. It can help us overcome."

RALPH

RALPH, 48, WAS BORN AND RAISED IN ST. LOUIS. A HIGH SCHOOL guidance counselor, he was divorced in 1984 after nearly eleven years of marriage.

"I met my wife, Cecile, in January 1973, proposed to her around March and married her in July that same year. We're both from St. Louis and we met at a community college where she was a student and I was a counselor. She was the friend of one of my students and I met her on a kind of blind date for a party. The relationship took off from there.

"At the time, Cecile was 20, eight years my junior. She had just finished her associate's degree that December, though I didn't know her at the time she attended college. She was working at a small manufacturing company out in the city and she told me early on that once we were married she would move into sales.

"We married, and I felt that things were going well for us. We purchased a house and got involved in a lot ̮ ̮hings that I thought she was enjoying, black movement things, basically, here in St. Louis. That continued for a while, but I have to say that I also had an increasing appetite for alcohol and it became a problem in the marriage. Cecile was aware of my drinking before we were married.

"In January '83, I went into the hospital to have my back worked on. While I was there, I began to detect some distance on Cecile's part, and my hospital roommate even made a comment about it. He asked if she loved me. So, when I got out of the hospital, I asked Cecile directly if she loved me. She said no, she didn't, and hadn't for some time.

"So, of course, from that point forward the relationship began to go down fast, although we stayed under the same roof for about the next nine or ten months. That period was like a living hell. She said she needed her distance, her space. But I later found out that this "space" had already been occupied by somebody else. Up until the time I went into the hospital, I thought things in our marriage were fine. But I should of known something was going on. That fall, Cecile had given me a case of the crabs. She blamed it on a brush which had been laying around the backyard pool area. Since I was unsuspecting, I didn't question her further.

"My wife kept her unhappiness within. We didn't argue at first, and I tried to save the marriage. To help with my drinking problem, I entered an alcohol treatment program here in St. Louis that uses a kind of therapy where a patient gets all the alcohol that he wants, and then is injected with some stuff that makes you sick. It made you feel that you hated the smell, taste and sight of alcohol. I haven't had any alcohol since I finished the whole program in May 1983.

"Interestingly enough, I think Cecile could basically handle me when I was drinking, but as I sobered up and began to want to take charge of things, I discovered the crucial thing that she had hidden from me. It was that she had determined that the marriage was over and she wanted me out of her space so she could get another person into it. Eventually, we divorced.

"Before we did, though, Cecile got a restraining order to get me out of the house. We had gotten kind of physical in the last few weeks before that; it was something like she baited me. She wanted a means of getting me out of the house. I have since learned that this is a common tactic used to get a man out of the house—have the woman bait him. And if he touches her, or anything to that effect, a woman can get a temporary restraining order.

"The order puts you out for about two weeks and then the woman goes back to court to get an extended restraining order that lasts for six months. When that six-month period elapsed our attorneys decided we didn't really have to go through another extension. So, instead we filed for divorce and had it seven or eight months after we had separated. It was quick in, quick out.

"But it was a nasty divorce. We have a boy, 14, and a girl, 12, from the marriage. They remained with Cecile, but I see them quite often. When I want to arrange to see them, I contact them. I won't contact my ex-wife directly. It's sometimes difficult, but what I do is leave a message on her tape recorder. She's remarried, and she and her husband are in sales, and they have a business phone and a private phone, but I don't even know the private number. I leave my messages on the business number.

"Cecile's new husband is not the person she was dealing with when we broke up. Instead, she married a brother who's in the Nation of Islam, who has eight kids, each from a different woman. To my knowledge, she hasn't joined the Nation.

"One of this man's sons has moved in with them and my kids. His son, who's nine, is sharing a room with my son and he still pees in the bed. The man has a 13- or 14-month-old child, and others ages two, five, nine and thirteen. And a few more who are grown.

"After my divorce, I had a few relationships, three that were long term. They got me back into the dating game, which turned out to be...madness. Boy, there are some crazy folks out there, some humdingers! The first one I encountered was a young lady who I worked with when I was a counselor. She was a divorcee with a young daughter. I would characterize the relationship I had with this woman as rocky, and I'd characterize her as somewhat manic depressive.

"I lived with another sister—let's call her Susan—from January 1986 to September that year. This was a strong sister. She was raising her son alone and had gone back to school. She had been single for some time, and wanted to get married. But I wasn't ready at that point because I was only two years out of my own marriage. Susan broke the relationship, I think, because I didn't respond fast enough for her. It was probably for the better because she had a very hot temper and she would simmer when she got mad, rather than talk. She also didn't relate to my kids too well. But we parted on good terms.

"In fact, I broke up on good terms with all my girlfriends I had since the divorce. It was only the breakup with my ex-wife—and we had a pretty nasty one—that did me in.

"Then there was Martha, who was very self-centered. It was almost like she was making up for something that she missed out on as a teenager. Maybe some attention, I don't know. But she had this need to be out there, like a socialite, a star. She was very, very self-centered. But our relationship lasted for two or three years because there was some good sex between us.

"But I got tired of other things about her. Sometimes she tried to beat me down, and I told her, 'you're a bitch.' And I don't generally call women bitches. But I told myself, I don't have to tolerate this shit for a little piece of ass. Even a good piece.

"Martha liked to pick arguments, and nitpick. She was moody, and I finally had enough. We may have had some super-duper sex, but I thought about what I had to experience to have that. I asked myself if it was really worth it. It wasn't, so, I ended that relationship.

"Now, I've been with a young lady named Ethel. In fact, we've been living together since the summer of 1989. We met at church. She has three grown daughters and the youngest, who is about 21 or 22 is going to move in with us.

"Things have been going pretty fine with Ethel because she's settled, she's not trying to prove anything to anybody. And she doesn't have this whole need to be on center stage all the time, you know. It's just a mature relationship and like a breath of fresh air after all the bad relationships I went through. I'm caring for my 90-year old father, who has Alzheimer's Disease, and Ethel has been very supportive of me. Marriage is something that may eventually come up for the two of us, but we're not pushing the issue."

DANIEL

DANIEL, 25, LIVES IN DETROIT WITH TERRI, HIS WIFE OF THREE years. He recently completed a year and a half in the Air Force and is currently working as a machine operator at Chrysler Corporation before continuing his education.

"I've heard a lot of brothers say that black women only want you for your money. But there are a lot of lovely sisters out there, and I've been with some who are really nice. Then again, some of them do want you for your money. I guess you have to take your time and get to know a person instead of just jumping into things.

"Before I was married, I had some good relationships with black women, and some not so good. I dated one sister from the Bahamas when we were going to the same high school. She was a very dark skinned, very beautiful sister. Because of her looks, a lot of guys were always hitting on her. She was the kind of woman who really, really liked the attention. She'd always say that I was being jealous and that I had nothing to worry about.

"But if I were walking her to class, and some other guy called her name, she would just leave me and talk to him. Or, if I was over to her house and other guys would call, she would stay on the phone for hours. They'd also come over and see her when I was there, and she'd stay outside talking to them for a while. She expected me not to be mad about this. But that was just one case.

"I've been with sisters who I've treated with respect and I've been treated with respect in return, just like any relationship should be. I guess it just comes back to the character of a woman.

"I'm married to a Caucasian woman, and I was always comfortable with my marriage. I know that no matter what, I'd never turn my back on my people. If a sister asked why I married my wife, I'd sit down and explain that I just happened to fall in love with my wife. We were friends first and dated for almost four years before we got married. I got to really know her.

"I don't really get upset when people talk about my marriage. I guess people might look at the two of us walking down the street and say I've lost my identity or sold out black people, or something like that. But I always remind myself that unless a person talks to me or gets to know me, it's only his opinion; a person has to talk to me and get to know me to understand how I feel about those things. I love myself, and I will always love my people. And it doesn't bother me to be married to a woman who is white.

"We never had any opposition from her parents or my parents. I'm the youngest of three brothers and two sisters and we were raised by our mother. I was fourteen when my parents split up, but I saw my father a lot and we always talked about things.

"Neither of my parents raised me to date just one particular type of woman. They always gave me my space so I could find out what I wanted. I dated European, Caucasian, Arab, Hispanic and Oriental women. They all had some of the same, but also different, qualities about them. I always tried to get to know a woman first. I think no one should ever feel pressured to do something, or to not do it. If you really like a person for whatever he or she docs to make you feel good, then that's the person you should be with.

"I know that there seems to be some problems between black men and black women. I don't know precisely what the problem is. But I think sometimes we just need to sit down and discuss what's on our minds. That's the only way you get things accomplished—get things out in the open.

"Maybe we need to have forums to identify the problems because there are so many superficial things going on between us, games that don't make any sense. Black men and women shouldn't get caught up in them. We should sit down as a Black community and listen to each other without any yelling or screaming. I would love to be part of a forum once just to hear others' opinions, and to air my opinions.

"When I hear black men say black women are only after their money, I think it's just that they haven't given sisters a chance. And sisters will say that brothers are dating white girls because they'll do more things in bed. And that's just not true. Other brothers say that a white woman will treat them like a king. But I tell them that I've known some sisters who treated me like a king and I've treated them like the queens they were. All those stereotypes about black men and black women can go out the window as far as I'm concerned, because they don't allow you to get to know a person. If you keep these stereotypes in mind, you won't get to know the inner person, only what you see on the surface.

"The way I look at it, I just happened to fall in love with a Caucasian woman. But I know who I am and she can tell you herself that as far as things of my race are concerned, I identify with blacks. I will never, ever turn my back on my people.

143

I just couldn't do it. I'm always going to be black. And my people are black. That's where my heart really is."

FRANK

FRANK IS AN AFRICAN AMERICAN ARTIST WHOSE WORK IS exhibited around the country. He is married, and lives and works in Brooklyn Heights.

"Let me say first of all that I love all black women. But the problem I've run into is that the new generation of women— those between the ages of 30 and, maybe, 40- have listened too much to white women who talk about women's liberation (this started in the 1960s). A lot of things that are happening with our black women are really things that they're picking up from white women. We really should be picking things up from our ancestors. Unfortunately, I think that the white man is still in control of the black woman. And that makes her reject black men.

"When black women read magazine articles about the black male, we have to always remember that all of those magazines (except *Essence* and John Johnson's publications) are owned by white folks. And when we see programs on television that try to depict the feelings of black men and black women, we have to remember that those, too, are controlled by white folks.

"It's sad that some of our sisters, even some of our established sisters, will do anything for money and fame. Anita Hill is a prime example of that. I don't have anything personally against the sister, but I think the issue that she brought up about this brother [Clarence Thomas], eight years later or however much time it was—well, I think he was just simply trying to get a piece. His approach may have been wrong, but on the other hand, maybe she wanted to give it to him. It didn't work. Then the next time she saw him, he was with a white woman. So she was totally angry.

"But all in all, ain't nothing wrong with a black woman. As a black man, I could not live without them. And I don't mean screwing and all of that, but just to be in their presence. It's their energy that glows. All of the negative things we hear brothers saying about black women—it just ain't true. I mean, my mother is a black woman. And I'm married to a black woman. I've been married to two of them. My daughters are black women. They may do things that we black men don't like, but then, we do things that they don't like.

"But getting back to the changes going on with black women here—well, I see it in my life, I saw it in the past—I see it in the present, I see it in the future. But at the same time, I don't condemn a sister if she's got a job as an anchor woman on the news. That's maybe the only thing she could do. Sometimes, there are problems when a sister starts working as an anchor on the news, or becomes vice president of Pepsi or whatever. You know "the man" has already pushed her up there to make black men look like lesser men. At the same time, the sister don't ride the bus no more. That's why she can't meet no brothers. Or maybe she doesn't go into the areas where the brothers go. Just because the brother may be a bus driver or work for the sanitation department or something, doesn't make him a bad brother. What's happening to a lot of black women now is that they're not even going in certain circles anymore. So they ain't going to meet any brothers.

"But if a sister was to get on a bus and ride and talk to the bus driver, the bus driver would probably be a cool brother; even if he had a jheri curl. A sister can work on that. Maybe the brother needs some guidance, and maybe a sister could talk to him. Women shouldn't just say, "hey, he's negative and he ain't got it together and that's it." That's what a lot of sisters are doing today. When we go back to the African model, the Africans taught black women to be different. But somewhere along the line we've lost that.

"When you talk about the young black male today and what he's doing— with the shootings and all—well, there was a time when I was growing up, that somebody in the neighborhood who would whip our asses, especially the males, if we were doing wrong. I remember that. And the other brothers around my age remember that. Why ain't we doing the same thing now?

"If you go all over the country, you'll find that there are women's organizations, black women's organizations, white women's organizations. Very seldom do you find a black organization where men are talking about helping young men. Also, I've had the chance to ride with a lot of brothers, because I travel all over the country. Black men shouldn't just be talking about getting some pussy; we should be talking about some more positive things. If we're single, why ain't we talking about finding a nice woman to marry or to be with. I don't want to hear as soon as I get to Oakland, "Man, I hope I can find a nice sister to give me some pussy." That ain't what it's all about. I know if I was a fly on the wall of a car riding with two sisters, I'm pretty sure they wouldn't be talking about just getting some dick where they're going. They may be talking about meeting a nice brother or something.

"The thing is that black men have stopped re-educating the young brothers and so we have problems. There are certain rap groups I can't deal with. But I don't blame the rap groups because a lot of the producers are black. A lot of the people playing the music on the radio are black. If you put on music that condemns black women, and you're just doing it for the money, then you got a real problem. The way I see it, all this came from white women back in the 1960s when they said we'll liberate this and we'll liberate that. And, "let's change the amendment on freedom of speech" and all. Black folks don't need to be doing all of that because it creates all these problems with our young men and our young women, who get pregnant. And I can talk about young women being pregnant because I have a daughter that got pregnant twice. And I was home. But I couldn't deal with the [influence of] radio and television. I couldn't control that. There was no way.

"But now I have some grandchildren, and I'm going to make sure to control them, if I have to whip their asses all the way through. Because we've got to do something. I still think that it has to do with man-woman relationships. Do you know the most beautiful thing I see? A Black couple walking down the street holding hands. I mean, I get off on that. To me it's almost like me personally having sex, just to see that. And then when they say they're married, it just does so much more for me.

"There's so many negative things being said about the black family. Like, we don't get along, we can't work together. But me and my wife have run a business together. We don't always agree. And we argue. But ain't nobody saying "I got to leave because I just can't work with you or because you a nigger." We can do it. Sometimes we have to look at the Chinese, the Japanese and the Italians and see how they always kept their families together. We see Mexicans all over the country and the first thing we say about them is negative: "Damn, about 100 of them live in a house!" But they're pulling together for the betterment of their family—which again goes back to the male and female.

"That's the same thing we blacks need to do. To me, the answer still is that brothers my age—between 30 and 50, 60— need to start pulling ourselves together, start talking and find solutions for the young brothers. And when we find a solution for them, then we'll find a solution for the sisters."

ROBERT

ROBERT, 44, LIVES IN CHICAGO, WHERE HE WORKS FOR THE U. S. Postal Service. He was married for 21 1/2 years and, at the time of his interview, had been separated for a year and a half. He was considering divorce. This is his story:

"I met my wife Monica when I left Chicago at age 19 and moved to Los Angeles. We were going to the same school out there and became friends. At the time, I thought I wanted to be a disc jockey, so I was taking a course in broadcasting. Monica was studying to be a dental assistant. We were married in 1971, about a year after we met. She was 19 then.

"When we were dating, my wife did everything possible to please me. If I wanted to come over to her place and watch a basketball game, she wanted to watch, too. If I wanted to go dancing, that was fine with her. I knew that she was sort of shy and insecure in a lot of ways, but when she was around me, I seemed to help her.

"Within the first year of our marriage, a change took place. All of a sudden, when she felt bad, she would tell me to leave her alone. 'I will be alright,' she'd say. "I just need my space to myself. Just wait till I come out of it." Before, I was always the one to bring her out of that mood.

"I'm a very sensitive person, and consider myself a romantic. I like to touch, to hug a woman, and I want her to be a part of everything I do. Monica seemed to be saying she didn't need to do the things we had done when we were dating. Her attitude was, "I married you now didn't I? Now don't push it." I was still wanting a little more coziness between us but, all of a sudden, it was too much for her. Before we had even been married 10 years, she told me once (and it really stuck with me) that we didn't have to kiss when we made love anymore. That really, really hurt. It was like she had stabbed me.

"I told her how I felt, more or less. I told her that I thought what she had said showed that things were pretty bad. I guess that she'd been wanting to say it for a long time, and finally did. What she told me was, 'Well, we can do what we have to do, and we don't have to do all that hugging.' But I liked it all—the kissing, the hugging, touching. It was very important to me. So I knew I was facing a problem, and it was getting worse.

"A lot of the situation, I believe, had to do with the fact that my wife got heavy into religion as a Jehovah's Witness a year after we married. And she didn't play with this. She had a full-time job on which she had to work two nights a week, and then she had Witness meetings two other nights. On Saturdays, she went out and did service [as part of the religion], and then on Sundays she went to Sunday service. So she was doing some activity four days a week. There was just no room for me.

"It used to be that I was off on Wednesdays and she didn't go to work until 11:00 a.m. If we were going to have sex that week, it had to take place on Wednesday morning. I hated that.

I'm a spontaneous person—you can't schedule my sex. But I knew that was the one time that she would comfortably have sex. That's why I did go along with her, but I hated it.

"I also tried going to services with her, but it wasn't my niche. I think I did everything I could to try to make the relationship closer. And it just didn't work. So naturally, like most men, I entered into outside relationships because I felt I wasn't getting what I needed at home.

"After a time, Monica got a sense that I was cheating. In fact, she found out that I had loaned another woman some money when a check bounced. I told her then that she and I were just hurting each other, and things were getting bitter between us. I said I had a problem—which was, basically, that I needed someone who would give me some attention. I didn't say anything about wanting a divorce at the time. Or, that I wanted to leave her for another woman, which I didn't. I asked Monica if she wanted to help me, and I told her that I needed a different type woman than she was.

"Her answer was to tell me to go and get that type. She didn't realize that I was reaching out for her to change.

"I didn't leave Monica right then, but I did three months later. I tried to take care of things—bills and such—in an orderly fashion and was also giving her a chance to evaluate our situation. I felt that Monica didn't want me to go, but she also didn't think there was that much wrong with her. I was the one in the wrong because I was cheating. She wasn't. She was a Christian, a Jehovah's Witness. She was not having an affair. I was.

"I feel that if I had not had an affair, Monica would have been perfectly pleased with the marriage. Because, basically, everything else was her way. I didn't complain or protest about her or the kids going to Witness meetings.

"In the 3-month-period before I left, Monica did ask me if we could go to counseling. But I turned it down. Why? Because, for the whole twenty years that we had been married, I could never get Monica to understand anything that I was saying. I was basically saying, 'I need you.' I was saying that I needed more from her. I wanted my marriage to work, but instead of fighting for me when I said I needed a different type of woman, she got mad and said, 'go.'

"After I left home, I stayed with a sister of mine for about four months. During that time I met a woman in my bowling league, and we started out dating. I've known her now for about a year, and I've been staying at her place for the last 8 months. What's interesting is that in the year's time that I've been with her, I have not cheated on her once, nor had the desire to. I had only cheated in my marriage because I wasn't getting what I thought I needed at home.

"I found out that being with one person is really me—I could not be a playboy if I wanted to because I'd end up liking just one person. I thought that for a long time that maybe I just couldn't have a one-on-one relationship. But after growing and maturing, I realize I have much more substance than I thought I had. Being with just one woman is a great thing. I found out that not only can I do it, I prefer it.

"The woman I'm with now, Leticia, is five years older than me. I wasn't looking for anyone older than me, or any specific age. I didn't want anyone too much younger, because I felt that I had matured to a certain level. Leticia has been a big help to me—she's given me more substance. She also gives me the attention I want and need. She's the best sex partner I've ever had.

"The only problem that's come up is something that I didn't see at first: I can take criticism, but it has to be constructive. It bothers me for a woman to try to "front me off" in public, and Leticia will do that, occasionally. I'm sensitive, and wouldn't do that to a woman, so I don't want her to do it to me. I feel I love Leticia, I care about her, but it's something that bothers me. I've told her, 'You don't have to praise me for what I do; I'm not looking for praise. But don't go off on me, that's all I'm saying.' I don't believe a man should tell a woman when to talk, when to speak. And it's fine if she's smarter than me, or makes more money than me. Other men could look at her—it says I've got good taste. But we have to work together, side by side. If I'm treating a woman like a lady, honestly giving her my best, it bothers me for her to try to bring me down. If a woman does that, then I can't be all the man that I want to be for her. Leticia does this a lot. And it makes me feel bad.

"So I've made up my mind that I want to get my own place: When I first moved to California at 19, I lived with an uncle. Then I shared an apartment with a male friend. Then I lived with my wife for 21 years. After that, I moved in with my sister for four months. Now, I'm with Leticia. She's helped me, but I think I need some space of my own. I need to see what I want. I don't want to keep having relationships and end up blaming the women when things don't work. I really want to analyze myself, check myself out.

"The next relationship I get into has to be one of substance, or else I don't want it. I know I don't need [the relationship] and can't give anything to it if there's no substance. If Leticia can't control her tendency to go off on me, it's not going to work for us and I'll tell her that she may need to have her space to herself for a while.

"I feel I'm reaching maturity in stages. I've made some mistakes but I know I'm learning and benefitting from them."

CHAPTER NINE

COUPLES SPEAK

THE MOST RECENT STATISTICS FROM THE U. S. CENSUS Bureau indicate that marriage is out of fashion among African American men and women. Annually, the divorce rate for black men and women rises while fewer and fewer of those who are over the age of 18 marry. Still, a little investigation will turn up loving black couples of all ages from across the country who are committed to each other, their families and the institution of marriage. Even as their number dwindles, they provide black singles who want to marry with a positive picture of how it used to, and still can be.

Black married couples who maintain their union year after year have their own theories about what it takes to stay together. The reasons are as varied as the couples themselves but almost all of them mention the need for mutual respect and love and the ability to allow a partner to be individuals within the marriage. Four couples—recently married, married one year, twenty–two years and forty–four years—sat for joint interviews and spoke about their courtships, wedded lives, and discoveries about lasting relationships. Their stories:

THE JACKSON'S

TRACY SMITH–JACKSON AND ROBERT "SCOOP" JACKSON GREW up together on the same street, literally. They spent their childhoods together knowing the same people, going to the same corner store, attending the same block parties. In what has been considered an "urban jungle", Chicago, Illinois, Tracy and Scoop were able to find a friendship that this year turned into a marriage.

Tracy is a 26 year–old service manager for a Fortune 1000 company in Chicago. Scoop is the 30 year–old editor–in–chief of *The Agenda* magazine. Tracy holds a Bachelor of Science degree from University of Illinois while Scoop obtained a Master of Arts degree from Howard University.

Although they grew up together, they did not seriously consider romance until 1986. After dating for eight years, they were married October 14, 1994 in a small jump–the–broom ceremony in Chicago.

"It was special," Scoop says. "To me, the wedding was the perfect expression of black–on–black love. The ceremony was about more than Tracy and myself being united in marriage. It was also a reminder to everyone present that despite the statistics and the media hype about the poor state of the black family, every weekend in this country, black men and women are committing themselves to each other and to the creation of a strong family unit."

The newly married couple's transition from childhood friends to husband and wife was awkward, "to say the least," Tracy declared. "When we grew up Scoop was like a big brother. I had a crush on him like everybody has a crush on most of their older sisters and brothers' friends. But he always treated me like a little sister."

When they grew older, Scoop went away to college and lost contact with Tracy and her family for several years. They happened to run into each other by accident one night in the parking lot of a local corner store.

"I was shocked," Scoop remembers. I mean Tracy has always been cute—but now she was like 'grown–cute'. You know what I'm saying? Baby–Sis wasn't baby–sis anymore. It's funny, because I swear my perception changed immediately. It went from fun–loving brother to 'let's hook–up.'"

"He's tripping'," she replies. "I looked horrible. I was in my brother's car with some of my friends, hair in rollers. It was my sophomore year in college. My brother told him that I was in the car. He came over to the car and told me he was going to call me so that we could see each other. I knew then this was going to be a date as opposed to a buddy–brother–sister kind of hanging out like we did when I was little."

Although that meeting was the beginning of a romantic relationship between Tracy and Scoop, things did not go smoothly. The geographical distance between them became a burden, as did the importance of their friendship. One of the most difficult areas of concern for them was the fear that the friendship would be lost if the relationship did not work.

"One time I saw a friend of Scoop's at a party," says Tracy. "I was talking to her about him and I going out for New Year's Eve. She began to tell me about how 'Scoop has a different woman to go out with every New Year's Eve, and that I was just another one of his girls'. That bothered me on two levels; one because I thought I knew him as a friend better than that, and two, because of our new relationship."

"What bothered me the most about that," Scoop replied, "was the fact that it was a lie, and that Tracy never confronted me on it. I figured, above and beyond anything else, Tracy and I were close enough as friends for her to come to me about something like that."

Over the next few years the two would "drift" in and out of each others lives because they were never living in the same city at the same time. When Scoop returned to Chicago from school in New Orleans, Tracy was away at school in Champaign. When she graduated and returned home, he had entered graduate school in Washington, DC. In addition, there was always a differing sense of direction and focus between the two.

"When he was in school in New Orleans, he always knew what he wanted to do and what kind of relationship he wanted. At the time, I didn't know any of that," Tracy says. "It was intimidating to be with someone who was focused when you're not."

"And that's what I believe was one of my faults in our relationship," Scoop responds. "I was about to graduate and I already had a job. The only other aspect of my life that wasn't 'guaranteed' at that time was my relationship with her. Because even then, knowing that I could spend the rest of my life with her, was not good for her. In hind–sight, I think my 'focus' became a sort of sub–conscious pressure, which can be kind of messed up if everything isn't in sync."

In 1992 a different transition surfaced. After almost two years of not being in contact, Tracy decided to mail Scoop a birthday card. They were both living in Chicago at the time, but she neglected to include her address or phone number.

"Then on Christmas Day, I was in my front room watching a tape of Beauty and The Beast. When the tape went off, I heard Scoop's voice. He was on some talk show on T.V. discussing rap music," Tracy said.

"And what remains funny about that is, my cousin and Tracy's play–brother were sweating me to get in touch with her," Scoop adds.

"When we finally saw each other after the two years apart," Tracy responded, we had a long talk, got some things out in the open and cleared a lot of things up. We found out that we still loved each other and that we could still be friends, which was most important."

"Yeah," Scoop added, "that day was special because for the first time she and I really came to grips about what our relationship, as a whole, meant to each other. It was here I believe the 'sync' finally started to get right."

Not long after that the commitment to their relationship set in, they became best friends and lovers.

"For a while we never argued, and I almost thought something was wrong with that," Scoop claimed. "Not that I'm used to arguments, but things seemed too smooth."

"Sometimes I think it's too good to be true," Tracy added. "Sometimes I wonder why we don't blowup at one another or disagree a lot or why everything just rolls with us. But, I realized, that as long as we've known each other it's always been that way. We're both relaxed and go along with each other. The biggest arguments we've had, and they haven't been arguments, they were debates, have been over social issues. The most heated we'll get is arguing over Minister Farrakhan or something like that. It's not like we argue over anything."

Tracy also believes that the uniqueness in their relationship is nothing extraordinary. "I think people are so used to controversy in their relationships," she says, "and so used to not being happy that they think it's fine to be that way. They expect the extra drama to be there and it doesn't have to be. I think people are so used to everything going wrong, that they look for problems and they are really not trying to do anything different. And I don't think that it has to be that way."

One evening after seeing the movie "Aladdin" they decided to get married. Tracy claims that the entire event was "magical".

"The movie made the engagement and the wedding special," she says. So special that they used one of the songs from the movie in their wedding ceremony.

Now that all of the hype and hysteria are over, they've returned from the honeymoon and the bill collectors are back calling the house on a regular basis. Tracy and Scoop have found time to sit down and discuss their future on an honest and open level. Money, children and security seem to be at the forefront of their conversations.

"It's rare for us not to have children yet," Scoop says. Most people in our age range have kids, especially if they're married."

"I would love to have children, "Tracy adds, "but preferably not right away. Because right now, I honestly feel that I'm too selfish to have children right away. I just want to spend time with Scoop."

"To me that's not a characteristic of selfishness, it's a characteristic of focus," Scoop interrupts. "Part of the problem with some of the kids out here now is that the people that had them were not ready to have them, let alone raise them. Tracy and I will be damned if we fall into that. We take having and raising children seriously. The problem is a lot of people fail to do that."

"Our first real vacation together just happened on our honeymoon, and we've known each other for years," Tracy continues. "There are a lot of things I want to do and a lot of places I'd like to go with him and you can't do that when you have children. I mean, you can do it, but then you have to leave your child, and I know me, I wouldn't want to leave my child."

"I think this all goes back to the friendship," he analyzes. "Tracy is the only person in the world that I can spend days, weeks, months at a time with, and want to spend that time with her."

THE LONGS

WALTER LONG, 47, AND SANDY LONG, 46, NATIVE NEW YORKERS, have been married for 24 years and are the parents of two sons, 20 and 17. Walter works as a systems programmer for an information services company and Sandy is an assistant corporate secretary at the American Stock Exchange.

The Longs were attending different colleges in the city when they were introduced by mutual friends. Walter, who grew up in a city housing project, says that Sandy stood out from all the other girls on campus. "I used to see all these black girls on her campus and she was the only one I ever saw reading a book," he recalls. "I felt that she was going somewhere, whereas most of the women I grew up with didn't seem to be going anywhere. So I said to myself, 'okay, this is the one for me,' and the relationship went on from there."

About 20 years old at the time, Sandy did have a sense of purpose. "I didn't know where I was going, but I thought I was going to make it, because I'm a survivor," she says. "That's the way I was raised. I thought I could do anything. There are things that I may not get done because I won't take the time to figure them out, but I know I can do anything I set my mind to. I've always had some kind of direction."

Marriage and a family were something she had looked forward to, and Walter and Sandy were married the summer after she graduated from college. Both liked the idea of marrying early because they felt they could grow together. Sandy says, "When you're younger you are a little bit more flexible in terms of what you can deal and can't deal with. Older people are set in their ways and when they meet someone, it can be tough to change their lifestyles."

Both Sandy and Walter grew up in two–parent homes and neither of them lived on their own before they were married. "It wasn't like today where couples live together and are able to take vacations and go off together and kind of play house first," Sandy says. "When we first did those things, we did them together, as a married couple."

After they married, Walter and Sandy lived in Brooklyn in a four–story brownstone. Walter recalls that "there were four couples living there, basically dormitory–style. Some of them had children, and there were others on the way. It was fun for us living there." Sandy and Walter waited three years before they began their own family and they believe it gave them a chance to get used to each other. "I took on some of Walter's stronger points. And he maybe took on some of mine," Sandy says. All the couples in that first building they lived in kind of grew up together, but today, the Longs are the only one of the four couples still married to each other.

One of the things Sandy and Walter learned in the early years of their marriage was how to give each other the space they needed as individuals. "It's not that I 'allow' Sandy to have her space—she does what she's going to do," Walter says. "I can't tell her that she can't go someplace or that she can't see someone or do something she wants to. I think men lack maturity when they do that. I always wanted a smart woman, an independent woman, a woman who was strong and forceful; someone who could handle things on her own if I was not there and things needed to get done. I never wanted a stagnant woman, someone who would stay at home and mind the kids, barefoot and pregnant, the way a lot of men like to see women."

Sandy had to work out her feelings about giving Walter his space. "When we first got married, Walter would get on his bike on a Sunday and take off with a friend while I stayed home. I'm not saying I liked it. But I dealt with it, maybe because I didn't know any better. Or maybe because I didn't want to say anything. Another person might have said that Sundays were one of the days we had off together, and he was being irresponsible. But maybe at the time, going out to ride was something that he needed to do."

On the other hand, Sandy said there were things she liked doing, then and now, that Walter doesn't really care to do. "Walter never liked to party, whereas I'm a people person and like parties. It wasn't easy, but there were times when I would get dressed up and go out to a party with my friends. Walter and I had a lot of battles about that because he didn't want to accept it; it wasn't something he liked. I'm sure most men wouldn't. But he didn't want to go with me. So we faced the question of what to do about it. We've battled verbally about that for many years." Sandy says that although Walter never tried to prevent her from going out, "He'd be pissed off when I got back home. But this issue has worked itself out over the years and now it's not a problem. That's where the flexibility we talked about is really important. I go to a party if I want to, and I accept it if he doesn't feel like going. Now when I come back in he'll ask if I had a good time. No problem. But we grew into that. It didn't happen overnight."

In fact, the Long's marriage has been a continual process of learning about themselves, each other and their children. As in every marriage, there have been moments when one or the other has felt like they have "just about had it." Sandy says that at one point, when one of her sons was an infant, "I was finding out that all the things that Walter liked to do weren't the things that I wanted to do. He probably felt the same way. It was as if we had been living together a few years but we weren't 'on the same page.'"

Sandy thinks that a key to keeping a relationship together, even in rough times, is "starting off with something that's real powerful and real strong." She says. "Love is a big part of it, but I think respect is also major— respect with capital letters and fire works. Men and women have to respect the person that they think they love because that's going to get you through in the long haul. That's what Walter and I have had. And it was important because in a lot of ways we are not the same people. We are both the eldest children in our families. And so we're both very, very head strong."

Walter says amen to that, adding that he and Sandy are both "real independent" and like to do what they each want to do, when they want to do it. "And we each swear that we know the best way to do everything," Sandy adds. "I mean, down to putting on a doorknob. That could be a major thing in our household because, first of all, I already knew how to do it yesterday. And Walter's read six books on the subject, so he knows how to do it, too. So he'll have one end of the doorknob, and he'll stand on one side of the door and I'll have the other end, and will stand on the other side of the door. But we get it on some way. Now, it may fall off next week because of the way we did it, but I think that we respect each other's right to even think we know best."

"Walter and I are different in a lot of ways—the way we grew up, the way we were raised and even some of our philoso-phies—but I really think that he's the smartest, most intelligent male that I've ever met. And he's the best father I could have picked for my kids. Though we disagree on a lot of things, when times get hard, I have to go back to that thought. He's also a role model for the boys he coaches in baseball and football. Around the neighborhood he's known as Coach Long."

Family is important to Walter and he, in turn, compliments Sandy on her commitment to their children. "I couldn't have picked a better mother than Sandy for my children. That was one of the reasons why I was attracted to her. I think it's sad that so many young black men are growing up in homes where their fathers aren't around and they don't learn what it takes to build a relationship with a woman. Their ideas of relationships are formed by what they see in the street and what they see on television, on MTV."

Growing up in Brooklyn, Walter says, his father "was always around and he never mistreated my mother in front of my eyes. So I think the relationship was good. He was a role model in the long run." But, he says, his own relationship with his father was always poor because he looked at him primarily as an alcoholic who had difficulty keeping a job. Walter vowed that when he became an adult he would never do many of the things he saw his father do. "I basically strive for that everyday. Still, I miss him a lot since he passed away six years ago. I think we could really sit down and have a good conversation now. But I miss Sandy's father as much as my own since his death because he was more of a father role model for me after I was grown; we could always talk."

Sandy describes her father as an aggressive self–made man who worked hard to provide a home and security for his wife and two daughters. Her mother was a homemaker who had a deep interest in her children and home and was very much in love with her husband. She was shattered when her marriage ended after 23 years and her husband married a woman he apparently had a long–time relationship with. "It broke her heart," Sandy remembers. "She was not emotionally strong and she went downhill after the marriage ended. The experience made me see that loving somebody can be quite painful and can make or break you. Family has always been really important to me and I think that's what has kept me going in my marriage even when I've wanted to say, 'I can't deal with this, I've got to get away.' I always wanted children and a family environment for them to grow up in."

Elaborating, Sandy says, "Our sons are the nucleus of our marriage. I would be hesitant to say that we stayed together for the children, but I think in a lot of instances when times were tough, they gave us something to work together toward so that we could maintain a relationship. I don't think anybody should stay together just for the sake of the children. That's what my mother did and it was too painful—she ended up losing in the end. But if there's something already there—love, respect —and your children, then you build on that and the children are a very integral part of the union. I know a lot of couples whose kids are like pictures on the wall. The adults are really into doing for themselves and their children are like appendages— something that just happened along the way. For me and Walter, our kids are paramount. We'll do without to provide for them."

Walter speaks of his sons with pride: "Our kids never really ask for much and they've always done their best to do what they can for themselves. We've never had problems with them in school or in the street. Or at home. So when they ask for something, Sandy and I will go without in order to get it for them."

There are no problems with their children, but when other pressures from inside and outside their marriage create stress, Sandy and Walter worked through the problems themselves by talking. They've considered therapy, but have not gone. Walter says, "I think we probably should have; there are a couple of things that we have to work out that I think therapy might help because sometimes you need a referee. But we're both pretty private people and can probably do the therapy on our own if we really put our minds to it."

Sandy has reservations about seeing a therapist, though. "I'm not into therapy," she confides. She's reluctant to put her faith and trust in a person who is "just another human being." She asks, "How could they tell me how to live my life and what's best for me?" She adds that she doesn't get her strength "from other people because they can let you down...make or break you," something she finds "just too scary." Sandy considers herself a religious person (she's a longtime Sunday School teacher), but she and Walter have never even discussed their differences with a minister. "I'll admit that I'm the reason we haven't seriously considered therapy," Sandy says. "I went to a therapist through a program at work when my father died because I was feeling terrible. The therapist—a woman—was quite nice and I felt "up" afterwards, but the stuff that I told her is nothing I wouldn't tell anybody. It wasn't a secret. But then she had me fill out forms and I really got turned off because it seemed like just a business. I had no desire to go back and I never did after that one session."

Relying on their own commitment to each other and their family to keep their marriage going, Sandy and Walter have reached a stage where they are at ease with each other and have their own way of communicating and relating. "Yeah," Walter says, "we fight, we argue, we get loud and sometimes it's not real comfortable at home. But at least it's not a physical thing where I'm smacking her around or she's smacking me around."

What do they fight about? They agree that they disagree about money. "I'm terrible about handling money, really bad," Sandy admits. "Walter is great with money, but money's not important to me. I couldn't tell you what I have in my checking account now. If I had to handle the household accounts, everything would get done, but in a haphazard way. And maybe one month we'd be on the streets if it was up to me alone—not intentionally, of course."

So Walter handles most of the finances and tries to bring Sandy along in that area. Any other complaints? "She's always late. I mean, she's never on time. She doesn't pay attention to the clock." Sandy counters with the fact that "Walter doesn't do any housework." For example, she says, "we were planning a cookout recently and Walter was around the house, but a friend called and asked him to play paddle ball. Now, he knew we were having company and there were a lot of last minute things to get done indoors and outside. But he went off to play, and I was a little bit annoyed about it. I could have made a big deal about his leaving me to do the work, but I decided it wasn't worth a major fight. Either I was going to do the work or not. We discussed it later and I told him how I felt about the whole thing. He heard me out. I could have gone on and on, but it wasn't worth ruining the whole day. Sometimes, you have to save your fights for bigger battles."

As Sandy sees it, "a lot of our women have a problem with that idea because everything is a fight. But you have to work together to make it work; you've got to pull together, so when the big battles come, the two of you are not pulling in opposite directions. I think that the important thing for black women is to differentiate what those bigger battles are. If you don't make that distinction, everything becomes a confrontation." She adds, "It's hard for me because I'm headstrong and I always know I'm right and I never apologize. If I call Walter a son of a bitch, I mean it when I say it and I won't come to him later and say I'm sorry. But I have to show him in other ways that I really respect him and do love him. And we're going to do this thing. We're going to be in this marriage."

THE FIGUEIRAS

LESIA FIGUEIRA, 31, RUNS HER OWN MARKETING COMPANY, Ife Communications. Her husband, Vasco Figueira, 33, is a U. S. court officer. They have been married for four years and have a two sons, Vasco Ejike, 3 and infant Tekene.

Lesia and Vasco Figueira met six years ago at a party and though it wasn't love at first sight, there was an attraction between them and she gave him her number. "It was kind of a fluke," she says. "It wasn't like I thought, 'Oh, oh—this is the man for me.' Nothing like that." But they had their first date shortly after and Lesia happened to have quite a few of her many nieces and nephews over at her house that day.

"Just from the way he acted with the kids," she says, "I knew he was different. He was great with them, and the two of us have literally been together since that day. He didn't leave my house that whole weekend and practically the whole next week. We just clicked. It was like he was my soul mate. I felt like I'd known him all my life, like I'd known him before."

Actually, Lesia had a boyfriend at the time, who was away in

Jamaica. But Vasco was unattached. "I really didn't have anybody," he remembers. "I was just kind of out there, but we got along so well that things just grew from there. I liked Lesia because she was very down to earth. She laughed a lot and she didn't really have any hang–ups."

Lesia's positive feelings about Vasco were confirmed for her in the first couple of years they were together. Her thoughts turned to marriage. "I felt it was time," she says, "and I was getting a lot of pressure from my parents and girlfriends about getting married." But, she says, Vasco wasn't ready. "He felt like he wanted to make sure I was the right person," and he had his mind made up that he and Lesia would have to first stay together for three or four years before he would commit to marriage. Lesia agreed with the wait because "deep down" she thought it was best and she knew that Vasco was in the relationship "for the long term."

But the wait was still frustrating for her, she remembers, because Vasco was "still partying, still running around with friends and riding his Kawazaki 750 Turbo motorcycle," a bike which got him a lot of attention from women. With hindsight, Lesia says, she's glad her husband went through this period because "he got the partying out of his system."

Vasco maintained his own apartment in the first years they were dating although he was often at Lesia's place. They both knew they wanted children eventually and were happy when Lesia became pregnant after they had been together almost three years. But she lost the baby late in her pregnancy. "The experience was devastating," she says, "but really brought us together; we supported each other. That's when I really knew he was in my corner and that he was serious about our relationship and life together."

Lesia and Vasco had moved in together while she was pregnant. In spite of their tragic loss, they wanted a child and decided to try again when Lesia was well enough and had her doctor's okay. Six months later, she conceived. This time she had the guidance of Queen Afua, a nutritionist–healer in New York

City (author of Heal Thyself), who prescribed a program of proper nutrition, cleansing, meditation and fasting. When she was six months along in her pregnancy and feeling fine and healthy, Lesia and Vasco went by themselves to the island of Anguilla and were married on the beach at sunset. "It was a very spiritual ceremony," she remembers.

Both of them work at keeping their marriage harmonious. In looking around at friends and acquaintances, though, they see lots of room for improvement in relationships between black men and black women. Vasco believes that black women need to learn how to cooperate with the black men in their lives. "When I'm on the subway or walking on the street I hear women saying things like, 'I kicked his ass,' or 'I cursed him out.' This kind of talk and attitude has got to stop." On the other hand, he feels black men have a lot of problems and need to first learn how to live with themselves, by themselves, even if it means being homeless and living in the street. "Part of being a man is controlling your own destiny," he says, "whether it works out to be healthy or unhealthy."

Lesia and Vasco are both conscious of the way tension in relationships between black men and women affect families and the community as a whole. "It's very sad the way things are," Lesia says. "We've got to stop warring and sit down and learn to respect each other. Women have to realize that the men they're putting down are their men. They are the ones who are going to help them through their lives and they should not be called niggers, even in casual talk."

"There's a way black women have of saying, 'my nigger this,' and 'my nigger that,'" Lesia adds. She recalls that she called Vasco a nigger one time "and I couldn't believe it." Vasco was in another room in the house when Lesia made her comment to some girlfriends. "I was shocked and ashamed," she says, "and sorry right away that I said it. But it's so pervasive for us to look at our men as niggers. Just as it is so pervasive for black men to call black women bitches. Like in so many of the rap videos. Some rappers have no respect for women. And many girls have fallen right into the same mentality; they accept being "dogged" and talked to in any way. Some have been degraded so much, they don't even see themselves as women. They adopt the dress, speech and mannerisms of men. It's sad."

A part of the solution, as Vasco sees it, is for black men and women to demonstrate respect for each other. "If they do," he says, "then their children will see that there's respect inside the home; that will give them confidence and make them more able to deal with what's going on outside their home. If there's no animosity between the parents, everything is better for the children as they grow up. They'll think, 'hey, this is the way it's suppose to be...one day I want to be like mommy and daddy.' As our family values become stronger and we become stronger families, we become stronger as a community. But," Vasco warns, "a lot of this is not going to take place until relationships between black men and women improve."

He refers again to the way some black women talk about black men. "I've heard women without steady men ask their girlfriends who are in relationships, 'Why you cooking for him? Why you got to do his laundry? Why you got to do this? Why you got to do that?'" Vasco wonders why these women don't just mind their own business and allow women to do what they want to for their husbands or mates. "There are definitely things that a man is going to do for a woman that a girlfriend cannot and will not want to do," he says.

When Vasco was a student at Morehouse College in Atlanta for his sophomore and junior years after transferring from Tuskegee University, he heard a speaker address the weekly assembly of 2,000 young black male students. "This man spoke to us first about our lives, then about himself, then about our community and the issues we face. He talked about what the black man had to do if he was ever going to get his nation together. That speaker pointed out that besides talking about business, he wanted to focus on family. He said that every other race of man thinks about family unity except the black man. He said that with other races, the women don't sit around and bad mouth their men like black women do. Our women will sit around and dog black men out for hours."

Lesia agrees that black women tend to put black men down: "Male bashing is so prevalent among us. Women get together just to 'dish the dirt.' You'll hear one sister ask another, 'girl, what did your man do?' There's a lot of negative talk."

Vasco considers the bad–mouthing evidence of self hatred. "If a woman is not going to love her man then she really can't love herself. And if we don't love each other, the race cannot continue," Vasco says. "I think it comes down to the fact that woman don't really want to follow us. It's partly the fault of black men because we have not really understood that it's our responsibility to lead."

He continues, "White women have the longest life expectancy in this country, longer than white or black men and black women. They are revered as the symbol of beauty in this country. Why? Because her man is in charge. If your man is in charge, what do you have to worry about? He's going to take care of you. That's the way it's supposed to be. Instead of black men and black women fighting each other, there has to be a way for the black man to be propelled to the front. There are sisters walking around who don't give a second thought to what's going on with their men. A lot of them say that we men are just belly–aching and it's time for us to stop complaining. In a way, they're right, but in another way women have to have compassion and realize that they have to get behind their men. I don't mean behind them like second class citizens, but if a man is out there working and his woman is bringing more money into the household, she cannot feel, all of a sudden, that she has power over her man or can degrade him. This happens a lot of the time. I'm the man of my house; my wife can go out and make three times as much money as I make, but that's the way it's going to be."

Lesia found that it wasn't easy for her to adjust to Vasco being in charge. "It's been hard for me, in our relationship, to just say 'okay, you make all of the decisions, and I'll just follow,'" she says. "It is very difficult. I mean, Vasco and I could sit here on a high horse and talk about what's needed in the black community, but the reality is that it is difficult to achieve these things and he and I have had to work out our own relationship. It hasn't been so simple. In fact, it's been hard. We have a vision of what we want out of our relationship— the way we want things to be, how we want to interact, how we want it to be between us. It's a shared vision. We know we want a peaceful life with two more children. We'd like to have a house one day and we'd like to relocate—maybe to Atlanta, or perhaps California."

The Figueiras look at their goals as relatively simple. "We have a joint consciousness and would like to do something cultural to help the black community, in a place where it may not be happening," Lesia says. "This is something we want to work towards. If we go off the track a little bit in the things we're striving for, we check each and say, 'hey honey, we're off the mark. Let's work on this.' Even with our relationship. For instance, with a new baby, some of the romance is not there like it was before, so again, I'll say, 'honey, let's get back on the track.' I find you have to sort of keep your eye on the prize, on your vision, at all times. There are outside forces—his friends, my friends, family, work—that are constantly pulling at the relationship. So, it's never easy."

Vasco and Lesia realize that this is something they can't avoid and outsiders have less influence now than they did in the beginning of their relationship, they agree. "They're still there, but we've been really able to solidify," Lesia says. Vasco adds, "We care about our family and our friends and we have to deal with them; we just have to learn how to keep them in perspective. We're always working on that."

THE McGEES

SCUDDIE E. AND SARAH E. McGEE ARE KNOWN TO MANY OF THEIR friends and close associates as Poppa and Momma McGee. They are both 65 years old, have been married for 45 years.

They are the parents of four, the grandparents of six. Dr.
Scuddie McGee is a psychologist who has a joint practice with
his wife and works extensively with children, adolescents and
adults in the U.S. and West Africa. Dr. Sarah McGee is an
Expressive Arts therapist and traditional healer, who studied
healing practices in Senegal, West Africa.

The McGees met in 1947 at a party given by a friend. By her
account, she almost didn't go. "Back in those days, parents were
very strict and I didn't have a chance to go to too many different places. I had a job as a baby sitter on weekends, and since
my curfew was 9:30 p.m., I didn't see the sense of going to parties. I knew I'd have to go home before the party really started."

But one week, a close friend of her father asked if Sarah
could come to his daughter's birthday party. He told her father,
"she never has a chance to go out with people her own age and
you know how strict you are; this would be a nice event for her
to come to."

The woman who Sarah worked for also thought that since
she was 17 and had worked for them on weekends for three
years, she needed time to have fun with her friends, so Sarah's
employer decided to give her Fridays off from then on.
Arrangements were made for her to go to the party.

Sarah wore a dress that she'd already had and when she got
to the party, she went into the kitchen to sit with the older
people. But they shooed her out, saying,, "Oh no, go on out
there with the young people—you're not going to stay in the
kitchen tonight."

Sarah remembers that all the girls at the party were dressed
up in their best and looked beautiful. She felt like a plain Jane
in her old dress, so she sat and watched everybody else dance.
The other girls were really putting on quite a show with their
dancing and flirting, but Sarah sat quietly. Sarah remembers
that at one point she looked over and saw a young man she did-
n't know with dark glasses on and an unlit pipe. The young
man, who was Scuddie, noticed her anyway and came over and
asked her to dance. Poppa McGee says, "Sarah looked differ-

ent than all the other girls there, had on a more old–fashioned dress. Although the others were more fashionable, after I met Sarah I felt there was something right about her." They danced another two or three dances and Ma recalls thinking that she liked him.

In spite of his air of sophistication, Scuddie had only learned how to dance at 4:00 that afternoon when friends showed him how to do the "slow drag." He was at the party as his sister's chaperon and the pipe and dark glasses were props to make him look cool: There was no tobacco in the pipe and Scuddie didn't know how to smoke!

After a while, the fellow who Scuddie had come with thought they should head for home, twenty miles away, and they offered Sarah a ride. Momma McGee says, "We sat in the back and held hands and he kissed me. From that day on the two wrote letters back and forth," between their New Jersey hometowns. Momma McGee still has and cherishes "every letter that he ever wrote me." Her impression of young Scuddie was that "there was just something about him that was different than the other young men. He showed respect and didn't come on as someone who knew it all."

The next day Scuddie told his mother that he had met a young woman who was a dancer and she's an artist, but his mother looked him straight in the eye, pointed her finger at him and said, "Just forget her."

Poppa McGee explains that the talented Sarah didn't fit into the plans his whole family had for him. "All my life I have heard, 'oh, you're going to be this, you're going to be that, you're going to be a medical doctor.' And I thought I wanted to be one, I guess because I'd heard it for so long."

In spite of a lack of enthusiasm on his mother's part, Scuddie and Sarah began to see each other when time allowed. He had begun college, she was completing high school and he would have to ride the bus to her home to visit her. Scuddie still remembers those visits. "Her mother would sit in the room right along with us. I used to wonder who I had come to see. Her mother had married at 15 so she hadn't had a lot of experience with courting. I'd get about 15 minutes at the end to talk to Sarah alone. Then I'd run and catch my bus. If I ever missed it, as I did several times, I'd have to walk home, about 20 miles away. What I'd do was walk as far as I could before I heard a dog bark. If I heard a dog bark, I would just camp out where I'd stopped. I slept outdoors many nights after I saw that I couldn't make my bus."

Though they had similar interests, the idea that Sarah didn't fit into the picture that his family held for Scuddie still was an issue. One weekend when Sarah was invited down to Scuddie's house, his mother had a scholarship dinner at their church to raise money for his education. (More than $25 was raised.) Without telling Sarah, his mother had also invited another young lady who was a classmate of Scuddie's at Monmouth College. But Sarah's feeling was that she liked him and not even his mother was going to separate them. They continued to see each other.

They married the year after the scholarship dinner, in December 1949, Scuddie continued college while working full time at a psychiatric hospital. It was to be 23 years of daytime work, classes at night and perseverance before Scuddie earned his doctorate.

Momma McGee says, "It was our belief that we could do it if we tried. Our children started to come, but we would scratch $250 together each semester for his education. We hear young people today who have to have a house, a car and the moon when they marry. We started in one room in a private house, with kitchen privileges. I remember that my husband's first paycheck was $52—for two weeks! We lived in that one room for about a year, then after our first child was born, we moved into a furnished house."

While Poppa McGee continued his studies and work, Momma stayed at home while her son was an infant and took some art courses. Later, during the Korean War, she got a job with the federal government as an engineering draftsman. "My husband and I pulled together— there was no such thing as my money, your money. We worked together."

She cooked simple, economical meals that would stretch a pound and a half of hamburger for several versatile meals, using tomatoes and cabbage and other vegetables from the garden they kept. A lot of Momma's friends were surprised at her domesticity. People would say "Girl, you still cook for your husband?" and she'd tell them, "Yeah, I cook for my husband." Momma McGee adds that she still cooks for Poppa today.

They were careful with their money in other areas of their life too. "I know that some people had French Provincial furniture," Momma reminisces. "Well, we had a convertible studio couch, two lamps and a table. That was it." Poppa recalled their first car. "It was a 1937 Chevy, that we bought in 1953 for $60. It took us everywhere we wanted to go. We drove it for about two years——until the ball bearings fell out of the wheels. Like a lot of cars built in its day, it had a wooden floor and if you went through a puddle, the water would come up and the car would start making funny noises, but kept going."

The McGees knew that other people, even their families, saw them as being different, but Momma says the difference is that "we had something that we wanted to do together." As in every marriage, there were times of stress. But the McGees can't remember real fights between them and they've only been separated to pursue educational goals.

"What we've always done throughout our marriage," Poppa says, "is to settle up before the end of the day. If anything went wrong between us, we would always talk about it before we'd go to sleep at night. We really would. Our biggest argument was over how many potatoes should have been cooked for supper. Coming from a family with 18 children, 14 living, Sarah was accustomed to peeling 10 pounds of potatoes."

He adds, "I think what also kept us together was the value system taught to us by our parents. My father was a Baptist minister and he, my brother and I were really great friends. We worked together as barbers in my father's same shop for 15 years. (Poppa worked Friday nights and Saturdays, in addition to his full–time job and studies.)

"Over the years, my father told me a lot of things, but one that I remember about marriage was that no matter how big a house you have, there's only room for one woman in it. We had our biggest problems when there was more than one woman in our house— once a niece that we took care of, another was a sister–in–law who came to live with us for a time. The worst times in our lives was when somebody else stayed with us. There was stress during one period because the way we and a visiting family member related to each other at one time had changed and we had to make adjustments for our everyone having aged and changed. Those words of advice from my father were a gift which really helped our marriage in touchy situations."

On the subject of how they managed to keep their marriage together, Momma McGee says, "I have great respect for my husband as an individual and I support all things he has tried to do in life. And he's always supported me. Recently, I was work-ing late at our office on some new jewelry designs and I looked out in the hallway and saw that Poppa had taken a pillow and was lying on the floor, waiting.

"I also have to thank him for encouraging me in my educa-tion. Things were sometimes very difficult because we had only "X– amount" of dollars to spend for our children's educa-tion but we'd manage to scratch together the money for me to go overseas. Some people would say he 'allowed' me to go on to Africa—I lived there on and off for nine years working on my doctorate, including nine months straight in 1986.

"During that period Poppa flew over to visit me, but before he arrived I wrote him a letter to give him expressing my love and happiness that he had faith in me. My husband was my first love, so I don't know anything about any other man. He is my only love. At the same time, back in America, he wrote me a letter and put it in an envelope for when we got together. While he was there with me, we renewed our marriage vows then exchanged letters. They were almost identical! That's the same theme that has run through our letter through the years." Poppa adds this about the cherished letters over the years from his wife: "Not only were they hot, they were perfumed. Each one carried her scent."

He also remembers that letter written to his wife during her extended stay in Africa. "It was a simple letter that dealt with the respect we had for each other and the fact that we could each express whatever we needed in our own lives. That's what has kept us together. We both have a sense of space and individuality. People used to ask me if I 'let' her go to Africa by herself? I'd tell them there was no way for me to let her do anything. She can do anything she wants to do. So, I guess that if there's a secret to a lasting marriage, that's what it is."

CHAPTER TEN

FINDING PEACE
THROUGH COUNSELING

THROUGHOUT THIS BOOK, NUMEROUS EXAMPLES OF relationship difficulties caused by self–defeating thought and behavior have been cited. These factors, often the result of unresolved emotional issues, play a part in most, if not all, dysfunctional romantic relationships.

Because of this, much of the solution to the Uncivil War lies in the resolution of individual emotional issues that hamper one's ability to maintain healthy relationships. In many cases, resolution requires professional assistance, either from a therapist or a trained pastoral or psychiatric counselor. In this chapter, mental health experts will explain a number of the common emotional issues that perpetuate the war between black men and women. They will also illustrate how counseling, either in a group or individually, can help resolve the relationship crisis.

RELATIONSHIP COUNSELING IN THE AFRICAN AMERICAN COMMUNITY

IN THE PAST, BLACK COUPLES SOUGHT OUT RESPECTED FAMILY elders in the community for help in finding solutions to relationship difficulties. Today, this honored tradition is rapidly dying away as more black families are separated physically and emotionally. Many black families now only come together on holidays or for family reunions. Young people often do not get to know their grandparents and older aunts, uncles and other relatives. As a result, the years of experience and valuable insights these elders have to offer is unavailable to far too many African American men and women.

That loss of contact has been keenly felt in the black community–the discord between men and women is one of its results. Without knowledge of the lessons learned and the strategies used by older family members to build and maintain relationships, many African Americans have little practical knowledge from which to evaluate potential partners. Nor do they have the experience or insight necessary to respond appropriately to situations and crises that occur within their relationships.

To compensate for the loss of valuable insights that once was obtained from elders, some African Americans are turning to psychiatrists and trained pastoral counselors. Unfortunately, however, the number of African Americans willing to seek professional help is relatively small. Despite the importance and personal benefits of improving one's mental and emotional health, many African Americans consider therapy and counseling "a white thing." A luxury for "neurotic, pampered Caucasians," they feel, that is irrelevant to and out of touch with black life and culture.

The irony of the rejection of therapy and counseling by African Americans is that we as a group need it more than most. Most psychological theories point to prolonged exposure to dysfunctional environments—primarily in one's youth—as the cause of emotional distress and confusion among adults. Since few environments are as dysfunctional as being black in a predominately white–oriented society, African Americans have a special need for mechanisms—extended families, churches, counseling—that help us cope not only with the difficulties and frustrations of life, but also with the irrationality of racism.

The impact of the messages of racism, especially the "inferiority" of African Americans, on the mental health of African Americans is the focus of a growing number of African American therapists and counselors. Through their efforts, there has been a pronounced change in how therapy for African American is viewed and conducted. Black therapists, trained in the classic psychoanalytic tradition of Sigmund Freud, Carl Jung and others, have adjusted these techniques to suit the realities of black life as it has been shaped by the pivotal, ongoing experience of racism. As a result, its level of effectiveness for African Americans has been greatly enhanced.

California psychotherapist, Dr. Derethia Du Val, says that black mental health professionals came to recognize that "we have to look at the African American experience in this culture, but we have to look at it from an African perspective." Black psychologists, psychotherapists, social workers, pastoral counselors and other mental health workers have begun, in Du Val's words, "to develop a frame of reference in which to verbalize and even think about [the black] experience in a different way."

As a result, black medical doctors and ministers are increasingly recommending individual and couple's counseling to their patients and parishioners. And now, more than ever, African Americans can use therapy and counseling to find healthful, effective ways to deal with the challenges of everyday life.

THE IMPORTANCE
OF SELF-AWARENESS

A NUMBER OF LICENSED BLACK THERAPISTS AND COUNSELORS were consulted for their commentary on relations between black men and black women. They are specialists who have for years listened to blacks talk about the difficulties and obstacles they face at home, on the job and in the larger society. These experts have heard firsthand what black women and men want, how they've been hurt, disappointed and frustrated. They have heard their hopes and dreams, both for themselves and for their children. They've gained insight into why the Uncivil War is being waged and how to bring about a cease-fire, if not peace.

There was widespread agreement among the experts interviewed that the first step toward building emotional well–being and healthy relationships is self–knowledge. This is a concept that is as old as man and is repeated in many world religions, philosophies and literature. Carol Meyers, Ph.D., an assistant professor of clinical psychology in the department of black studies at Ohio State University, put it this way, "Each person should take an honest look at himself or herself, and learn to love and accept that self. It's only after we can love ourselves that it's possible to love someone else."

Gregory Mathis, a social worker and therapist who counsels adults at a mental health care facility in the Chicago area, also sees a need for truthfulness in looking at self. "It's all about being honest with yourself and the other person," says Mathis. "It's about getting in touch with our feelings. We've got to say, 'I want to see the real you.'"

Mari Saunders, Ph.D., who is the staff psychologist for the Urban League in Brooklyn, New York, believes that self–examination is paramount. At seminars she holds for black women and men looking for partners or for improved relationships, her message is: "Get to know yourself, get in touch with all the things that dwell deeply within you." Saunders believes that women and men have to find out why they're angry, why they're secretive, and why they don't trust others. "The answer is within self," she says. "There is no blueprint, no technology that can give you answers. If you get to know yourself well, you'll know exactly what it is you want. You'll know what you can tolerate, what you'll put up with. It'll help you in choosing a mate because you can't possibly get to know another person until you know who you are."

CARRYING OUR CHILDHOOD INTO OUR RELATIONSHIPS

BECAUSE WE ARE BORN INTO FAMILIES AND LIVE WITH THEM IN our formative years, most therapists and counselors believe that a big part of getting to know oneself is examining one personal history—one's family and upbringing. Saunders contends that the demands made on a person during childhood, everything a child is exposed to—the good, as well as negative things like abuse alcoholism, injury, neglect and poverty—"all contribute to a child's vision of life, and they ultimately play a part in the way that a person acts and reacts as an adult."

Dr. Saunders and James Jones, Ed. D., a family therapist in Houston, both agree that examination of one's past is not easy. "It's difficult for black families to acknowledge painful events of the past like abuse and incest," Dr. Jones says. "Even now with all the stuff that's been in the newspaper and on television, many black families deny these things ever happened to them. Many black men would have us believe that this behavior is not a part of our culture, that it's something that just started happening."

But digging into the past is tough, Dr. Saunders admits, because "people have to go through a lot of painful crap that they didn't resolve when they were growing up; chances are that it's showing up in adult relationships and they don't want to make the connection." To move forward, Saunders says, "a person has to remember the things that actually happened to her or him as a child." She adds that "a person may need to go to their parents or someone in the family who is older and ask some questions about things that happened in their childhood."

Heru Nefera Amen, who holds workshops at a multiethnic men's project in Oakland, California, also believes that unresolved emotional wounds from early life are carried over into relationships. Amen is sure that part of his own anger, hurt and pain stem in part from his early family dynamics and his relationship with his mother and other family members. "I probably took much of my childhood pain," says Amen, "into every relationship that I've been in."

REDEFINING OURSELVES AS AFRICAN AMERICANS

GETTING A HANDLE ON ONESELF THROUGH INTROSPECTION and examination of one's past is an essential element in building relationships that work. Another important element is having realistic expectations of what to expect from a relationship partner. Developing the ability to communicate and share each person's hopes and desires with the other is yet another element in building good relationships.

Dr. Saunders advises the women who come to her couple's seminars to really get to know a man. "I tell them not to get carried away by the fact that a guy is sending flowers, making phone calls and saying the right things. Men, especially those who have been raised by their mothers alone, learn the art of manipulating women, of telling them what they want to hear," she says. "A woman needs to interview a man, find out where he's coming from. What are his relationships like? What about his parents, his friends? Does she know anyone else who knows him?" In addition to this biographical data, Saunders says women, and men for that matter, need to ask themselves what kind of treatment they want and expect from a partner: "Do they want someone for the long haul? Someone who is tolerant, someone sincere?"

Other areas prospective partners should be queried on are their views on issues like raising children, capital punishment, or cheating on taxes. Dr. Saunder's believes it's a good idea to know a potential partner for "four seasons" before making a decision about him or her because that length of time will give each a chance to see how the other reacts in different situations.

Therapists Du Val and Mathis believe that much of the difficulty between black men and women is due not only to lack of sufficient knowledge about their partners, but also to the tendency of many African Americans to look to white America for their "role models." Both Du Val and Mathis strongly advise African Americans to turn to the black community for ways to define themselves. "As black people, we have to label ourselves, redefine ourselves," says Mathis. "When a person tells you that you're ignorant, violent or stupid they're using psychological whips to label you. We can't wait for someone else to do it and we can't give anyone else permission to do it. We have to define who we are and what we are in terms of our masculinity."

Dr. Du Val agrees. "African American men are using a white male standard of what manhood is and they can't possibly attain that standing because the cards are stacked against them—it's the nature of power in this country." To compound this dilemma, Du Val asserts, black women are seeking men who fit "the white women's ideal."

Many African Americans, says Du Val, are confused as to "how to be black people in this world and it's affecting how we communicate with each other." In centuries past "Africans revered the image of the woman symbolically and physically. Women were an integral part of the development of the community." Now, she laments, "we're looking to someone else's value system to show us how to relate to each other and it doesn't fit our reality. Many young women look to the white value system for role definition," Dr. Du Val adds, "so consequently, they have lost the strategies that their mother had in terms of seeing a vast number of [available] men in the community."

Unlike their mothers and grandmothers, many educated and professional black women refuse to date black men whose career achievements are not equal to theirs. "Black women today somehow believe that the American dream is obtainable in its white form, not in the black form in which we used to obtain it and were quite comfortable with." As Du Val sees it, parents and grandparents are partly to blame because they have not helped black males and females to understand how institutional racism has affected their personal lives and dreams. Elders have also "failed to tell them of some of the support systems and strategies that we [previously] used in developing male–female relationships."

FINDING PEACE
ONE MAN/WOMAN AT A TIME

SELF–AWARENESS AND SELF–DEFINITION, AS WELL AS UNDERstanding the impact of institutionalized racism on African American men and women are important first steps toward building healthy and lasting relationships. But even with all

this understanding, black male–female relations are not necessarily going to go smoothly. Each gender, unfortunately, still
harbor long standing complaints and suspicions that make it
difficult for them to communicate, trust and share their feelings
with members of the opposite sex.

"The goal of most relationships should be to establish inti-
macy," says Dr. Mathis. "But in black relationships, the goal is
not to get hurt, not to be used. There has been so much hurt in
previous relations, people begin to take a self–protective stance
that gets in the way of their getting close. So the partners are
suspicious of others and afraid of being manipulated." Somebody is always trying to place blame for problems that come
up," Dr. Mathis continues, "but there's no right and wrong as I
see it. There are good choices and bad choices, and good things
happen when you make good choices, and bad things happen
when you make bad choices. And you're not wrong if you make
a bad choice, you just need to make another choice. If we keep
placing blame, the relationship won't work and a couple won't
come together and negotiate."

According to Dr. Du Val, women—and often men—are
looking for "a little tenderness, a little understanding, a little
appreciation and a little support from their mates." Money is
important in this economy, she acknowledges, "but a woman's
primary focus is on the non–tangible things that black men can
provide."

Dr. Saunders agrees. "Often satisfaction," she says, "has
nothing to do with a man's sexual prowess—a woman wants to
be held, she wants to be caressed. She doesn't want to be nailed
to the wall and pounded to death. She wants affection, someone to scratch her back, hold her in his arms and talk to her. A
woman wants someone she can establish some kind of intima-
cy with. Somebody who can cry on her shoulder if he's upset
about something, someone who doesn't mind sharing the
god–awful thing that may have happened to him at work. But
many black men won't do this. They are too into their macho
things and that's too bad."

"Whatever happened to loyalty, faithfulness and understanding?" Dr. Saunders asks about black relationships. "We've forgotten how to be civil to each other, how to be nice to one another. Couples would rather have a confrontation than stop for a minute and recognize the ramifications of what they've done or said. They don't know how to back off, or think that maybe their mate has had a hard day. They don't consider the kind of background he or she comes from. If your mate is in a foul mood, it's not always a personal thing. But people like to establish that they are right, rather than consider that maybe the other person just got up on the wrong side of the bed that day."

"The problem is," Dr. Saunders continues, "everybody is talking, but nobody's listening. People want you to listen, to give a little sympathy. [Black men and women] can't see each other as enemies," she says. "They can't even see the large white society as an enemy because that doesn't work anymore—it just makes you the same as the people in that society. But a black man has to look at the black woman as his friend, someone who cares about him. Each needs to look around until they find someone who takes them pretty much as they are, someone who fits their idea of the kind of person they want, and vice versa. Blacks need to say to each other 'you and I are in this together.' We've got to trust somebody—who better to trust?"

Relationship counselor Amen has a similar view. "African American men have to recognize that our sisters are not our enemies," he says. "They're wounded too. They're hurting. Many of them have been knocked around and beat up and put down. But we've got to acknowledge that both of us have some healing to do and we can't blame our sisters because they're getting their asses kicked, too. A few black women seem to be making it, but the number is really marginal. They are the exception, not the rule. We need to recognize that."

In the past, Dr. Du Val points out, black men were very supportive of black women. "The biggest feminists in America were black men," she says. "The black women's club movement got a lot of support from African American men who wanted upward mobility for the race. They understood that the racial issue superseded the sexual issue and every able body in the community had to uplift the race."

Today, many black men and women can barely communicate with each other. Dr. Du Val's experience has been that couples who come to her often have never talked about their expectations of each other. To counter this, she encourages couples to talk about how it feels to be a black man or black woman in this culture, and then about what they are looking for in a mate. "We're not raised to talk about things like that," Du Val says, "and often black men and women don't know how to ask for what they need from their partners. So I find women complaining about men not talking to them, and men complaining that women don't listen to them. Basically, they're saying the same thing. It's about being able to communicate your feelings and risking vulnerability. Many young people have no frame of reference or vocabulary to explain where they are at and what it is they are feeling."

Amen also speaks about the need for better communication between black men and women. "They're speaking two entirely different languages," he says. "And their ears are basically closed. So I think we have to find a common language as African–American men and women because we have much healing to do among ourselves. We have to begin setting up dialogues that get beyond rhetoric. We've got to talk and listen to one another in a really deep way."

Therapist Carol Meyers also believes that one of the keys to building a successful relationship is communication. Dr. Meyers encourages relationship partners to talk honestly about their hopes, dreams and desires so that neither makes assumptions about what the other wants or needs. Couples also need to "bring a sense of fun to their relationship—they should laugh together." They should also work at developing nonverbal understanding and should also nourish the loving, sexual side of their relationship. Meyers feels that mates should work toward the development of their spiritual selves. She suggests that black couples "encourage each other to look inward and reach for a higher self." What is most important, Meyers emphasizes, is there must be commitment. "If a couple decides that they are truly committed to their relationship, they can work through whatever obstacles they may encounter."

Like Meyers, Dr. Saunders also believes that black men and women need to focus on reaching their whole or higher self. "It's not so much about finding the right mate," says Saunders, "It's about becoming the right mate—finding yourself first and understanding what it is you want. Couples often get together thinking that all the deprivations of their childhood can be satisfied by their mate, but that cannot be. No one can come as half a person looking for the other half. Each partner has to come as a whole person and then enhance, and be enhanced by, the other."

AFRICAN AMERICAN RELATIONSHIP THERAPY IN ACTION

SO THAT AFRICAN AMERICANS MAY ACQUIRE A BETTER UNDER-standing of what happens in the therapy process, as well as the greater understanding of self and relationships that come from it, two eminent black psychologists, Dr. A.J. (Anderson James) Franklin and Dr. Nancy Boyd Franklin, have agreed to take readers inside their relationship groups. In this section, readers will not only be exposed to the issues discussed by men and women in group therapy, but also how the therapy process works.

Relationship Therapy for Men

A.J. FRANKLIN, PH.D. IS A PSYCHOLOGIST IN NEW YORK CITY, offering individual and group therapy. He is also a professor of clinical psychology at City College of New York and is a co–editor of *Research Directions of Black Psychologist* published by Basic Books. His new book, *The Invisibility Syndrome of African– American Males,* will be published in late 1995. In the late 1960's, Dr. Franklin helped develop the Department of Psychology at the University of Lagos in Nigeria. He is also a founder and past president of the New York Association of Black Psychologists.

In his own words, Dr. A.J. Franklin talks about the benefits, results and process of counseling African American men:

"It's pretty classic that black men have difficulty seeking therapy as a help. It's not traditional for our folks to see a therapist, a counselor, or a psychiatrist when we have personal problems or some form of personal distress. Usually, we will go to our minister, a close friend or relatives. We'll even confide in our family physician rather than think of going to a mental health specialist. Some of that is changing, though. Having been in this business for over 25 years, I think the whole country is becoming more sophisticated about using therapists, and as mental health services become more demystified and have less stigma, the use will grow.

"Nancy [Boyd–Franklin] and I started groups out of our personal experiences in therapy, as well as experiences from friends. We thought that people needed to understand that they were not alone in the experiences they were having. We wanted them to know that they could bridge the trust or confidentiality gap and be able to open up with other brothers (or other sisters) about the kinds of personal struggles they were having. They could open up about daily life, their pain, indignation and vulnerability.

"We thought that if men in groups, and women in groups could share these things with each other and feel safe, they would learn that they're not the only ones in the world struggling. It could lead to a validation of their experiences as African American men and women which is really important for our sanity and survival these days.

"Most of the men in the first group I formed were college educated or above, so we're talking about middle–class professional men. They have many dreams and hopes riding on all that education and there are a lot of expectations put on top of that by significant others—parents, wives, supervisors, etc. So when men get to the point of coming into a group, I know that they have been pretty well worked over. I've gone through this myself and I've seen it in the issues men have brought into individual, family and couples therapy.

"When men come into a group I tell them it's a support group, a place where each can share his thoughts and feelings about what is happening to him as an African American male in a very racist society—a place where men can look at how that impacts on their lives personally and professionally.

"The original group of men that I gathered met for eight years. In the first week, we just dealt with their images. So they had to be willing to come in and risk their images. My task was to try to maintain a level of trust that would get them beyond the image stuff and down to something more serious.

"I told them that the group was not only about discussing experiences of African American men, but also about empowerment, which is problematic for black men in a racist society. The questions we would discuss were how they wanted to deal, where they wanted to go, what their personal goals were, their visions.

"Trust and confidentiality became the big issues because some men did not immediately see the merits of a therapeutic support group, or discussing personal concerns while looking at other men. Brothers, face–to–face; it's not how men see themselves. There's the whole macho, self–protective thing we all have. Coming to therapy is an admission that you're hurting. That suggests you can't take it like a man or that you must have something weak in your character. For many men, therapy is not consistent with the male image.

"Relationships were [also] an area we talked a lot about, especially the expectations of women they were involved with and the issue of commitment. The men have often discussed the hot topic of 'commitment–phobia' and whether they can fulfill the responsibilities of commitment, given the expectations of women and given the realities of day–to–day racism.

"Many men feel that after 'the search', 'the chase' and the courtship of a woman, the demands they get from women are unrealistic. Some men in the group feel they are not ready to commit because they aren't secure in their careers. Others hesitate because they are not certain they want to settle down with one woman. This is a big struggle for some men. We've talked in group about their confusion over how they can express continued interest in other women, once they have made a commitment; how do you handle past relations and casual attraction? Men don't want the kind of grief they can get from the woman in their life if they don't handle these other attachments tactfully.

"Something else that has come up in group concerning male–female relationships is how to deal with heated battles–not physical fights–but with serious arguments. Men are concerned about whether they can contain themselves when women get 'up in their faces' and say things that are provocative. They worry about crossing the line from verbal to physical confrontation. If they're arguing with men, the argument will be verbal up to a point, then they literally, or figuratively, 'go outside'. But with a woman, the argument just escalates with men not knowing how to finally settle it. Some men in group–and their wives–have had concerns about their being physically intimidating.

"There is a real issue with men in group about the anger that comes up in a confrontation with a woman you love. Most of the men are not as concerned about violence as they are about frustration. It seems too that women don't appreciate the fact that they have a boiling point. But men know that they have to contain their emotions in a conflict with a woman, and we talk a lot about what this does to them.

"Additional conflict and tension arise between men and women over certain expectations that women have of men, like making phone calls or showing up at agreed upon times, or fulfilling their commitment. There are also tensions around the career and fathering. Most of the men in group have talked about how they did not have fathers who were significantly present in their lives; either they were not present at all, or they were in the home but too busy with their work, or they were emotionally inaccessible. The issue that some men in group grappled with was how to be a father when they were not fathered.

"We dealt with many tough issues like these in my initial men's group. Men in the group said that it became essential for them to attend. Group was a place where they could express their thoughts and feelings and get perspective on them from brothers they could trust who were going through the same thing.

"The result for the men was greater awareness of their behavior and responses. They did not necessarily go through radical change, but with awareness, they had the choice of making changes.

"After I brought that first group to an official close, I formed another. I think groups are needed, just as individual therapy is needed. Black men are caught in a web of experiences where we're faceless and nameless, like the character in Ralph Ellison's classic novel, *Invisible Man*. It's what I call the invisibility syndrome. It's through my years of experience, not only as a black man but also working with children and families, that a model of therapy came together for me. One of the more psychological experiences for African American males is that you are essentially a nameless, faceless entity wherever you go. The paradox of this invisibility is that when you are visible, you are often seen as a threatening object. You are the victim of stereotypes. In different ways, black women are also viewed through the lens of stereotypes.

"As black people we have to live in spite of those realities. What I've seen in my work with African American males is a struggle to negotiate an invisibility and visibility seesaw with racism as the fulcrom. It grates on the gut, saps your strength. It becomes forever a part of your thoughts; you are always trying to figure out what is wrong with this picture here or in which ways you can handle this stress.

"In group I talk about the need to be clear in your own self–definition and anchor it in reality and a spiritual base. For me, that's an African American legacy. We have a history, and there are many things to be proud of: just surviving slavery and generations of racism, for instance. Not many people can be ripped away from their homeland and learn to survive in a hostile environment.

"My objective in group and individual therapy is to empower men to fulfill their visions, and I believe the route to empowerment is self–definition. The fact that black men can come in, sit, and talk about their lives is an indication, I think, that they are proud warriors. To me, black men who come to group therapy are reconnecting with their inner strength, their resiliency. That is the essence of surviving the daily rigors of being an African American man in today's society, knowing yourself, and the inner strengths that you need to succeed in spite of barriers."

Relationship Counseling for Women

NANCY BOYD-FRANKLIN IS A PSYCHOLOGIST WITH INDIVIDUAL, family and group practices in New York City and New Jersey. She is also a professor at Rutgers University's graduate school of Applied Professional Psychology in New Brunswick, N. J. The author of *Black Families in Therapy: A Multi-Family Approach*, she has also coauthored, with her husband A. J. Franklin, the forthcoming book, *The Children, Family and AIDS*.

To provide insight into the workings of the group therapy process, Dr. Franklin agreed to share some of her experiences in working with black female therapy groups:

"Black people today are very isolated. Often, they may be living some distance away from the folks they grew up with. Working in a white world, they don't see people they know and they have a disconnected feeling. I found that many of the black women I was working with had no network. Their extended family was either someplace else or had so many dysfunctional components that the women were trying to distance themselves from them; they had to find a family of choice— new people to connect with.

"I started group therapy with the idea of connecting people in a way that allowed them to give each other positive support. Women in the groups I've worked with have supported each other through divorce and through abortion. They have also supported each other through good events: weddings, christenings, pregnancies and births.

"One rule in traditional groups is that a therapist does not associate with the people in the group outside sessions. From my Afrocentric perspective, that just negates the purpose. I encourage the group to interact outside, but to bring their interactions back to the group so that members get feedback on how they are in the world. When a person comes to talk to a therapist individually, that therapist doesn't have any sense of whom she or he is in the world. So others who see her outside can tell me, that person and the group how she appears in another setting.

"There have been women who chose not to associate with any of the others outside and wanted to keep their being in therapy very private. That's their choice. In working with groups it's really important to keep confidentiality; all of the women are very clear about that.

"I think black women, and men, have been given a lot of victimizing messages by society around racism, economic issues and oppression. We've internalized many of these messages and we bring them to the table in our relationships. So one of the purposes of the group, in my view, is to challenge those victimizing messages. Take the notion of the shortage of black men: There are messages that go along with that notion that say there are no black men available or there are no good black men available. These are myths. What I want to do in group is to find a space in which black women can support each other in challenging these myths and victimizing messages.

"I had a woman who was being battered (her family had a multigenerational history of battery) come to group. Her family was encouraging her to stay in the relationship. 'At least he provides—brings home the paycheck,' they said. And, 'He did father your youngest child.' What the group does in this kind of situation is to provide a different support system so that she might break the pattern of abuse. The group provides a sort of holding environment in which a woman can get caring and support and a challenge to the way things are perceived. A woman doesn't have to use the myth of a man shortage as an excuse mechanism for abuse or as a justification for staying in an abusive situation.

"Discussions about the shortage of black males are always lively in groups of black women. Many younger women are despairing of ever having the chance to have relationships. But I find they sometime overlook the men who are in their lives.... I treat many black men who have told me that they have felt rejected by black women because they were simply nice men—not sexy or exciting and not college graduates. They were just regular nice guys and women overlooked them. This is an issue that comes up a lot in group when we talk about a man shortage.

"Women also come in with other issues. Our women have a lot of burdens on their shoulders: Marriage, children, relationships, caring for elders, caring for extended family and for non-blood relations. Healthy functional black families have always picked up non-blood relatives along the way; whenever we moved to a new area, we created a new family.

"Another purpose of the group is to help folks who are in the middle of extended families figure out how to be connected to them but without drowning in the process. I've found that many of the women I've seen, regardless of their age, are central in their extended families. Their extended families can be smothering unless we find a way to stand up for ourselves.

"I'm a family therapist, so we do a lot of work on the family of origin in group; we work on healing the wounds that so many women have. Often, they go back and talk over issues with their families. Others write letters to family members with the encouragement of the group. Sometimes they have to be given the strength to recognize that they can never give their families what they want. It's very painful to have this realization, but it has happened. What they have to do is build a family of choice.

The group also helps women look at the ways in which we replicate our family of origin drama in our current relationships.

"The groups I lead are ongoing and open-ended—people come in at different times. This is very powerful, from a therapeutic point of view, because you have a mix of people who are in denial, people who are almost ready to complete and others who are completing. That way, a person who is in denial gets challenged by people who are in different stages along the way.

"We do a lot of work on challenging myths, especially 'the black man ain't shit' and 'there's no good black man out there' myths. We also do a lot on the many negative messages we hear about ourselves as women——the ones about skin color, weight and body type. Our African heritage displays itself in many ways that don't fit the mainstream. Women in group have told some very sad stories of the messages they were given as girls about their femininity or lack of it, their intelligence or lack of it, their beauty or lack of it.

"If you ask a bunch of black folks what our socialization practice is, they will chant out: 'We raise our daughters but we love our sons.' White folks don't get this. They think this is simply sexist (which it also is), but they don't get that there are protective reasons why this has been done, that it happened to compensate for the bullshit that goes on in this society against black men.

"In the black community the perception is that black men are on the bottom. Black women are ingrained with mixed messages: On the one hand we are given a message to protect the black man; not to do him wrong in public, as Anita Hill did to Clarence Thomas. At the same time we hear messages that the black man should be in a position of power. He should be taking charge of this and that. He should not be the last hired, the first fired. But I think our women are angry from their socialization experiences where many of their mothers favored their brothers. That's why messages about protecting black men create rage in some black women. And the rage gets carried over into their relationships.

195

"I feel very strongly that the things that keep black women and black men apart are partly external but are also partly our own internalization of negative, victimizing messages about each other that have been laid on us by a Eurocentric society. If we can get to understand this, I believe that much more understanding would occur between black men and women.

"It's not that black men and black women can't communicate. I feel that you have to help them 'tease' out the part of it that is just their relationship, and the part that is bigger than them. This is very hard for black people because we are not socialized to express inner feelings. They are kept very private in our culture.

"Our families give women other very victimizing messages about relationships with men. They tell us on the one hand, 'God bless the child who has her own,' meaning we should be able to take care of ourselves, to raise our children and be educated so we can get a job and provide for them. But at the same time we're given the message that we should have a man, but keep in mind that there's no such thing as a Prince Charming.

"While women are hearing these things, men are given the message that they need to be assertive, aggressive, providers. But not too assertive because this society might kill them off. They're told they shouldn't let a black women get up in their faces and be assertive with them.

"So, I see many couples who have a clash of messages. They wonder, 'How are we supposed to do this? Are we supposed to do this like the white folks do it? Are we supposed to do it like on the Cosby Show? Are we supposed to do it like our mothers and fathers?' I mean none of this seems to fit. The model of relationships is, for some of our folks, nonexistent. They have modeled themselves on the mainstream that doesn't work.

"The world and relationships look very different if your man is perceived as on the bottom of society. Even a man with a Ph.D., like my husband, A. J. [Franklin] is fine as long as he's in his three-piece-suit and carrying his briefcase. But if it's a Sunday morning and A. J. goes out to get his paper with his cutoffs and his "X" cap, white people will not get on the elevator with him. So his vulnerability as a black man, and his vulnerability in terms of raising our sons and daughters is very painful.

"Black couples in relationships have to deal with the fact that they are both under a lot of pressure because of racism and they sometimes have to work not to let racism win. Instead of pulling together against it, couples sometimes take that pressure out on each other.

"In my groups we've looked at and talked at great lengths about situations in which people encounter subtle discrimination and racism. In my view, the purpose of a group is to have women who are working in a variety of settings in which racism is denied, get some support around the issue. Let's label it; say this is what it is. Let's name it so a woman doesn't take it personally. Group can enable women who are screaming 'racism' to look at what part is racism and what part is them. That has been a very powerful piece of intervention for folks.

"In general, I find that black people are being forced back to their spiritual roots. It is happening with women in particular (but also with men), as a way of coping with the realities of subtle, yet painful, racism. When I started in this field, spirituality was treated as if it were religiosity.

"Many of our women who were raised in families with a strong spiritual sense went through a strong period of rebellion somewhere in their teens and 20s and rejected the whole baby with the bath water. Often, crises later in their lives center around their spirituality, and we do a lot of work on this in group. I have also seen a lot of couples who have used their spirituality to rise above the problems they have to deal with. It scares me that there are folks treating our women, men, couples, or families who don't understand our spirituality.

"Another thing that we've had to work on in group is the fact that we're not trained to talk with each other about subjects like competition between our men and women. For example, whose needs come first? When and how do you balance the needs of each? One of the biggest issues for everybody, not just black folks, is that relationships are very stressful because of a lack of time. People are working longer hours in order to survive in the midst of this great depression. Folks are working much longer hours than they used to, so there's much less time to nurture a relationship. In group we also deal a lot with the issues of making time for oneself, for one's own life. Women are looking to learn how to get nurturing in a relationship, how to choose somebody who is nurturing.

"I see many women who are withdrawing from relationships. They're opting for celibacy. I heard one woman say: 'I've been wronged so many times I'm afraid. I'm just convinced I'm going to make another mistake—so I won't even try.' A lot of younger, professional women are despairing of ever having the chance to have a relationship. That's the internal dilemma that we have to deal with. I'm hearing this from some men, too.

"The group addresses these feelings, and what I find so positive about the groups is that I see growth and change. I have to feel that to do this work and I don't think it's delusional. I find that the women in group get the support, love and the power they need to go on. That's true of men too. They say that for the first time they feel understood."

FINDING PEACE
THROUGH EMOTIONAL HEALING

THE THERAPISTS AND COUNSELORS INTERVIEWED FOR THIS chapter prescribed a number of recommendations for improving black male/female relationships. These recommendations included increasing one's awareness of self and addressing unresolved emotional issues that lead to irrational thoughts and behavior. They also included making better and more rational decisions when choosing a rational partner.

Nurturing and developing one's spiritual side was also strongly recommended; as was developing the ability to listen and to communicate our wants and desires to our partners. Readers were also warned of the danger of defining themselves and other African Americans by standards set up by the larger society which do not take into account realities of black life in America.

None of the recommendations in this chapter will be easy to fulfill; old habits are hard to break. But the acceptance of these ideas is vital because the health of the black community is only as good as the emotional health of its members. The legacy of slavery and racism is more than just poverty, it is also wide-spread low self–esteem. And if one can not love themselves, how can they love another?

"As Africans we're going to always find ways to be together, says Dr. Du Val. "What we have to look at is healthy ways to be together. The beginning of that is dialogue and if we have to holler and scream at each other for the next two years, we need to do that. We need to sit down regularly—on a weekly or month-ly basis—and talk to each other about our pain, about our joy, about our anger, about our fears and about our frustration. It's just going to have to happen on a very large scale." And soon.

FOR REFERRALS:

IF YOU ARE INTERESTED IN LEARNING ABOUT HEALING THROUGH counseling and therapy, contact the organizations listed below or check with community mental health centers and hospitals in your city or town for additional information about where to get reputable help.

American Association for Marriage and Family Therapy
Suite 407, Department E
1717 K St., N.W.
Washington, D.C. 20006
(They can provide the name of private practitioners)

Association of Black Psychologists
P. O. Box 55999
Washington, D.C. 20040–4999
(202) 722–0808
(Callers and correspondents will be referred
to a practitioner in their area.)

National Association of Black Social Workers
642 Beckwith Ct., S. W.
Atlanta, Ga. 30314
(404) 584–7967
(The association will give callers the location
of local chapters which can make referrals.)

Black Psychiatrists of America
P.O. Box 370659
Decatur, Ga. 30037
(Write for information.)

American Association of Pastoral Counselors
9508A Lee Highway
Fairfax, Va. 22031
(Write for information.)

SELECTED READINGS

RELATIONSHIPS AND FAMILY

Billingsley, A. (1992) *Climbing Jacob's Ladder:*
The Enduring Legacy of African–American Families.
Simon and Schuster

Davis, L. (1993) *Black and Single: Meeting and Choosing*
A Partner Who's Right For You. Noble Press

Hooks, B. West, C. (1991) *Breaking Bread:*
Insurgent Black Intellectual Life. South End Press

June, L. (1991) *The Black Family: Past, Present, Future.*
Zondervan

Long, C. (1995) *Love Awaits: African American Women*
Talk About Sex, Love, and Life. Bantam Books

Hopson, D.S. and Hopson D.P. (1994) *Friends, Lovers,*
and Soul Mates. Simon and Schuster

Madhubuti, H. (1990) *Black Men: Obsolete, Single,*
Dangerous? Third World Press

Wallace, M. (1978) *Black Macho and The Myth*
of the Superwoman. Dial Press

COMTEMPORARY AFRICAN AMERICAN ISSUES.

Bell, Derrick (1992) *Faces at the Bottom of the Well: The Permanence of Racism.* Beacon

Cole, J. B. (1993) *Conversations: Straight Talk With America's Sister President.* Doubleday

Diggs, A. D. (1994) *The African American Resource Guide.* Barricade Books

Driver, D.E. (1992) *Defending The Left: An Indivdual's Guide To Fighting For Social Justice, Individual Rights and The Environment.* Noble Press

Edwards, A. and Polite, C. (1991) *Children Of The Dream: The Psychology of Black Success.* Anchor.

Hutchinson, E.O. (Ph.D.) (1994) *The Assassination of The Black Male Image.* Middle Passage

Lee, M. Soloman, N. (1990) *Unreliable Sources: A Guide to Detecting Bias in News Media.* Carol Publishing

Parham, T.A. (Ph.D.) (1993) *Psychological Storms: The African–American Struggle for Identity.* African American Images

Pieterse, J. N. (1992) *White on Black: Images of Africa and Blacks in Western Popular Culture.* Yale University

Reich, R.B. (1988) *Tales of A New America: The Anxious Liberal's Guide To The Future.* Vintage Press.

Russell, K. Wilson, J. and Hall, R. (1992) *The Color Complex: The Politics of Skin Color Among African Americans.* Harcourt Brace Jovanovich, Publishers

West, C. (1994) *Race Matters.* Vintage

Wilson, W. J. (1987) *The Truly Disadvantaged: The Inner City, The Underclass, and Public Policy.* The University of Chicago Press

AFRICAN AMERICAN HISTORY

Bennett, L. (1984) *Before the Mayflower.* Johnson Publishing

Du Bois, W.E.B. (1903) *The Souls of Black Folks.* Knopf

Hughes, L. Meltzer, M. and Lincoln, E. (1956) *A Pictorial History of Black–Americans.* Crown

MAGAZINES

American Visions: The Magazine of Afro–American Culture
The Visions Foundation
P.O. Box 37049
Washington, D.C. 20078–4741

Being Single: Magazine for Singles
Harbon Publishing
P.O. Box 49402
Chicago, Il. 60649

Black Enterprise Magazine
130 5th Ave.
New York, New York 10011

Black Scholar Magazine
P.O. Box 2869
Oakland, Ca. 94609

Dollars & Sense Magazine
National Plaza
1610 E. 79th St.
Chicago, Il. 60649

Ebony Magazine
820 S. Michigan Ave.
Chicago, Il. 60605

Emerge: Black America's News Magazine
1500 Broadway
New York, N.Y. 10036

Essence Magazine: A Magazine For Today's Black Woman
P.O. Box 51300
Boulder, Colorado 80321–1300

Jet Magazine:
820 S. Michigan Ave.
Chicago, Il. 60605

The Black Collegian Magazine
1240 S. Broad Ave.
New Orleans, La. 70125

The Crisis Magazine
260 5th Ave.
6th Floor
Brooklyn, NY 10001

Upscale Magazine
P.O. Box 10798
Atlanta, Georgia 30310

Young Sisters & Brothers (YSB) Magazine
1700 N. Moore St.
Suite 2200
Rossalyn, Va. 22209

INDEX